Eyewitness
CAT

Jaguar

Serval

Plaque showing a crowned lion, Limoges, 12th century

Tabby cat

Tigers

Eyewitness
CAT

Abyssinian kittens

Written by
JULIET CLUTTON-BROCK

Abyssinian

Ocelot

Maine coon

Black
leopard

Ginger and white cat

Puma cub

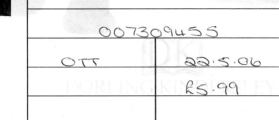

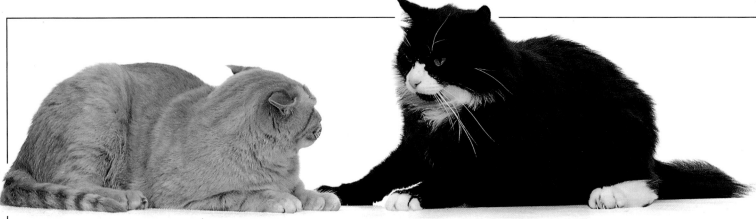

Ginger cat

Black and white cat

Bobcat

LONDON, NEW YORK, MUNICH,
MELBOURNE, and DELHI

Project editor Gillian Denton
Art editor Thomas Keenes
Senior editor Helen Parker
Senior art editor Julia Harris
Production Louise Barratt
Picture research Diana Morris
Special photography Dave King
Additional special photography Philip Dowell,
Colin Keates ABIPP

PAPERBACK EDITION
Managing editors Linda Esposito, Andrew Macintyre
Managing art editor Jane Thomas
Senior editor David John
Project art editor Joanne Little
Editor Sarah Phillips
Art editor Rebecca Johns
Production Luca Bazzoli
Picture research Sarah Pownall
DTP designer Siu Yin Ho
Consultant Kim Bryan

This Eyewitness ® Guide has been conceived by
Dorling Kindersley Limited and Editions Gallimard

Hardback edition first published in Great Britain in 1991
This edition published in Great Britain in 2004
by Dorling Kindersley Limited,
80 Strand, London WC2R 0RL

2 4 6 8 10 9 7 5 3

Copyright © 1991, © 2004 Dorling Kindersley Limited, London
A Penguin Company

A CIP catalogue record for this book is
available from the British Library

ISBN 1 4053 0547 9
Colour reproduction by Colourscan, Singapore
Printed in China by Toppan Co., (Shenzhen) Ltd

See our complete
catalogue at

www.dk.com

Early Greek gold
necklace plate

Lion

Puma

Contents

Leopard

What is a cat?

CATECHISM
In Christian communities, cats have always represented both good and evil. In this 19th-century illustration set against an industrial background, good and bad cat spirits fight over the soul of a cat woman.

Cats are possibly the most beautiful and graceful of all animals. They are sleek, have fine fur which is often strikingly marked with spots or stripes (pp. 14–15), and elegant heads with pointed ears and large eyes. The wild cats and the domestic cat all belong to one family, the Felidae. Although they vary in size from the common house cat to the huge Siberian tiger, they look alike and behave in similar ways; a tiger rolling in the grass looks very like a giant tabby (pp. 26–27). The cat family have all the typical features of mammals: a protective skeleton, an upright walk, a four-chambered heart, mammary glands which secrete milk to feed the young, and they are warm-blooded. Cats are amongst the most successful of all carnivores, or meat eaters, and they almost all live and hunt on their own. This solitary life is possible because cats prey upon animals that are smaller than themselves and are therefore not too difficult to kill. The exception is the lion (pp. 28–29) which hunts in a family group or pride. The domestic cat is one of the most popular of all animal companions because it is affectionate, intelligent, and playful.

NOW YOU SEE ME...
This jaguar is well-hidden. The striped and spotted fur of the cat family provides very effective camouflage in the great variety of habitats in which cats live. Both stripes and spots blend in well in forests, jungles, grasslands, or plains.

ACCORDING TO THE GOSPEL
The beautiful Lindisfarne Gospels, were written and decorated in Saxon Northumbria in Britain, around A.D. 700. The domestic cat was clearly a familiar sight around the countryside at this time.

The narrow stripes and tabby markings of this domestic cat are inherited from its wild ancestor

ADAPT AND SURVIVE
Domestic cats are very adaptable. They can live in a room, a barn, or a palace, and they are found all over the world from tropical Africa to lands of snow and ice, such as Greenland. The domestic cat is the only member of the cat family that lives and breeds happily within human society, although the cheetah can be successfully tamed.

Whiskers are organs of touch and help all cats, big, small, wild, or domestic, to feel objects in the dark

JAPANESE CAPRICE
In certain religions such as the Islamic and Buddhist faiths, cats have had a far happier history than in Christianity. The Japanese have a definite sympathy with the mysterious cat, and have often indicated its changeable nature by portraying one cat made up of many.

The mane of the adult male lion, is the only obvious sign of sexual difference in the whole cat family

CO-OPERATIVE CAT
The lion is the only social cat. It lives in a shared territory with other members of its pride and hunts on a co-operative basis. This enables it to hunt herd animals bigger than itself, like antelopes and zebra. Lions, like all cats, kill their prey by stalking and then leaping on it and biting into the neck (pp. 28–29).

All cats have claws and all except the cheetah sheathe them when at rest (pp. 42–43)

THE CAT THAT WALKED BY HIMSELF
The British writer, Rudyard Kipling, explained the cat's place in human affection and its need for solitude in a wonderful story called *The Cat that Walked by Himself.*

The first cats

MILLIONS OF YEARS AGO, many cat-like animals strode the earth, some more massive and fierce than any alive today. The cats are the ultimate in carnivore evolution, but many of the descendants of the early cat-like animals were smallish carnivores. The earliest fossil ancestors of the cat family come from the Eocene period, some 50 million years ago. These evolved into the species of large and small cats, like the lion and the domestic cat, that are living today. Another line of evolution produced the now extinct, sabre-toothed cats, so-called because the very enlarged canine teeth in the upper jaw were like daggers, and the cats used to kill their prey by stabbing them with these weapon-like teeth. Like the living cats, there were large and small sabre-toothed cats. The best known is the American species *Smilodon*.

STUCK ON YOU
In the Ice Age, a natural eruption of black, sticky tar at Rancho La Brea, now part of modern Los Angeles, trapped thousands of different animals, including 2,000 sabre-toothed *Smilodon*. These carnivores probably became trapped when they rushed into the tar after prey which were trying to escape from them.

Tooth root extends some distance into the skull

Very large teeth for biting off chunks of meat

Huge sabre-teeth used as daggers to stab prey

THYLACOSMILUS
Thylacosmilus looked rather like a sabre-toothed cat, but it had nothing to do with the cat family. *Thylacosmilus* was a pouched mammal (the young develop in their mother's pouch after birth) that lived in South America during the Pliocene epoch, about 5 million years ago.

Continuously growing upper canine tooth

Development of lower jaw into a bony sheath, protected large canine teeth

Artist's impression of Thylacosmilus

SUITABLE MONUMENT
Sir Edwin Landseer (1802–1873) sculpted the lions that flank Nelson's column in London's Trafalgar Square, to commemorate British victories in battle, like Nelson's naval victory at Trafalgar. During the last Ice Age, real lions roamed the freezing landscapes of Britain in search of prey like bison and wild horses. The bones of these extinct lions have been found right underneath the Landseer lions in the heart of modern London.

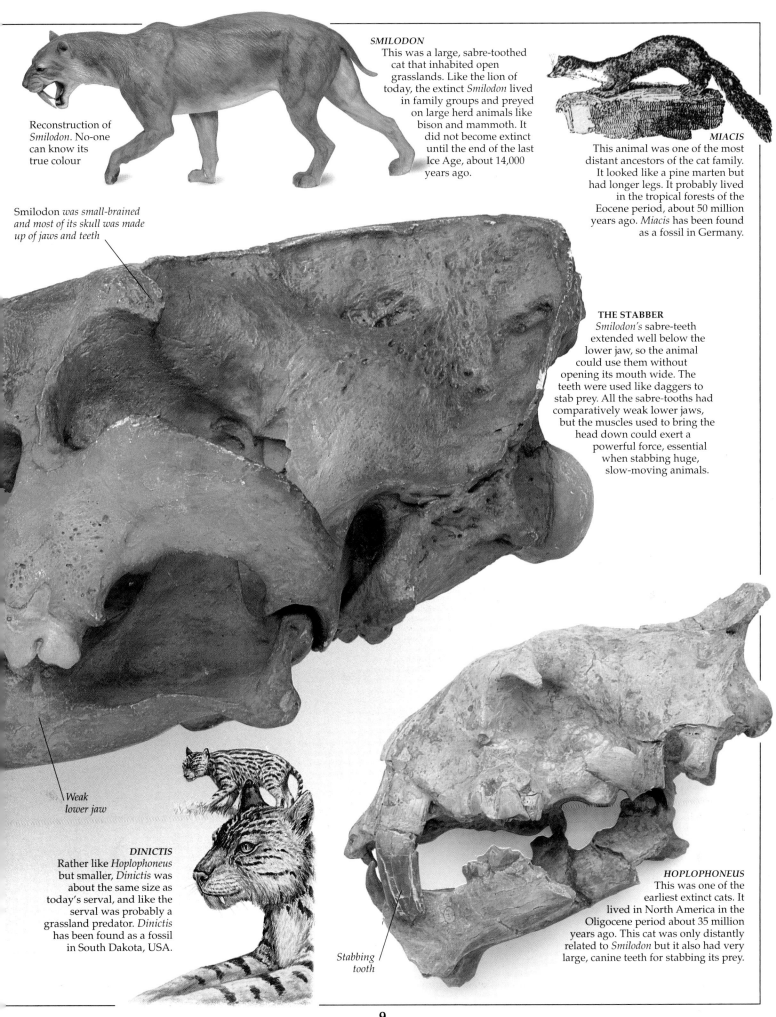

SMILODON

This was a large, sabre-toothed cat that inhabited open grasslands. Like the lion of today, the extinct *Smilodon* lived in family groups and preyed on large herd animals like bison and mammoth. It did not become extinct until the end of the last Ice Age, about 14,000 years ago.

Reconstruction of *Smilodon*. No-one can know its true colour

MIACIS

This animal was one of the most distant ancestors of the cat family. It looked like a pine marten but had longer legs. It probably lived in the tropical forests of the Eocene period, about 50 million years ago. *Miacis* has been found as a fossil in Germany.

Smilodon was small-brained and most of its skull was made up of jaws and teeth

THE STABBER

Smilodon's sabre-teeth extended well below the lower jaw, so the animal could use them without opening its mouth wide. The teeth were used like daggers to stab prey. All the sabre-tooths had comparatively weak lower jaws, but the muscles used to bring the head down could exert a powerful force, essential when stabbing huge, slow-moving animals.

Weak lower jaw

DINICTIS

Rather like *Hoplophoneus* but smaller, *Dinictis* was about the same size as today's serval, and like the serval was probably a grassland predator. *Dinictis* has been found as a fossil in South Dakota, USA.

Stabbing tooth

HOPLOPHONEUS

This was one of the earliest extinct cats. It lived in North America in the Oligocene period about 35 million years ago. This cat was only distantly related to *Smilodon* but it also had very large, canine teeth for stabbing its prey.

Cat clans

CATS KILL OTHER ANIMALS for their food, which means that they, together with about 200 other species, including bears, pandas, dogs, hyenas, raccoons, and weasels are all part of the order Carnivora (flesh eaters). There are four genera (or groups) within the cat family: the small cats, which cover 31 different species including domestic cats, and cats as diverse as the small black-footed cat and the large puma; the large cats (the lion, the tiger, the jaguar, the leopard, and the snow leopard); and two groups consisting of only one cat each, the cheetah, and the clouded leopard. Cats have remarkably well-developed senses, fast movements, and very sharp teeth, and are the most highly specialized meat eaters of all the carnivores. Wild cats range over every continent in the world except for Australasia, and there, they have been introduced by humans. The small cats differ from the large cats not only because they are smaller but also because they are unable to roar. The domestic cat is descended from one species of small wild cat, *Felis silvestris*, which today is still found in parts of Europe, western Asia and in Africa.

ORIGIN OF THE SPECIES
Carl von Linné (Linnaeus), born in 1707, was a Swedish botanist. He invented the system of giving Latin names to plants and animals. He called the domestic cat *Felis catus* and the lion *Felis leo*.

PUMA
The puma, or cougar, is an over-sized small cat that can purr like a tabby. It lives in North and South America. The first European settlers thought it was a lion but couldn't understand what had happened to the mane!

BOBCAT
This inhabitant of North America looks rather like a lynx without the long ear tufts. It is the most common wild cat in North America but is still seldom seen.

Small cats

Small cats include all the smaller wild cats as well as the domestic cat. All the small cats live on their own and hunt by night. They are found all over the world in a great variety of habitats, and tragically, many have been hunted almost to extinction for their beautifully patterned, soft furs.

DOMESTIC CAT
Today, there are nearly as many breeds of domestic cats as there are breeds of dogs. They are all descended from the wildcat.

Big cats

The big cats are at the top of the hunting pyramid, and require a great deal of meat. This means they have always been fewer in number than the small cats, who are more easily able to find sufficient food for their needs.

TIGER
The tiger is the largest and heaviest of all the cats. It is a night hunter, preying on animals smaller than itself. Tigers are found from tropical India to icy Siberia.

ON THE AIR
The lion has often been used as a symbol of quality. One of the best known advertising cats is the MGM lion, seen here practising his roar.

Odd cats out

Two members of the cat family are distinct from all others – the clouded leopard and the cheetah. The clouded leopard is a large animal, but it does not roar like the other big cats, nor does it groom or rest like a small cat. The cheetah is unique because it is a running cat (pp. 42–43), whereas all others are leaping cats.

CLOUDED LEOPARD
The clouded leopard is about the size of a small leopard but is not closely related. It lives in the forests of Southeast Asia but is rarely seen and is in danger of extinction. Like the true leopard, it often climbs trees.

CHEETAH
The cheetah is unlike all other cats, because it does not have sheaths over its claws and it can run at great speed. This ability is an adaptation to life as a hunter on the grasslands of Africa, where there are many other competing carnivores.

Ancestors of early cats

Social hunters · Solitary hunters

Leaping cats · Running cats

Lion · Other big cats · Clouded leopard · Small cats · Cheetah

THE DESCENT OF THE CAT
The relationships and fossil history of the different cats are not fully understood. In this diagram, the cheetah is separated from all the others and is called a running cat because it is unique in being able to chase its prey at great speed. However, it still kills it in the same way as all the other cats by leaping on it and biting into its neck. All other cats are called leaping cats, because they slowly stalk their prey and then leap on it.

The bare bones

THE SKELETON, CONSISTING OF ABOUT 250 BONES, provides a rigid framework for the soft parts of the body, protecting them from shock and injury, and at the same time allowing the cat to move with great agility and suppleness. The skull, in both the large and small cats, is highly specialized for killing prey and devouring it in the shortest possible time, before other predators can steal it. The eye sockets (orbits) are large and round to allow a wide field of vision, the hearing parts of the skull are large, and the short jaws open very wide. Cats kill their prey with bites from their very sharp canine teeth and then cut pieces of meat off with their carnassial (shearing) teeth. They do not chew their food, but bolt it down, nor do they gnaw at bones, so they do not need as many teeth as dogs.

NIGHT PROWLER
This snow leopard, hunting at night, reveals its fearsome teeth as it gets ready to attack.

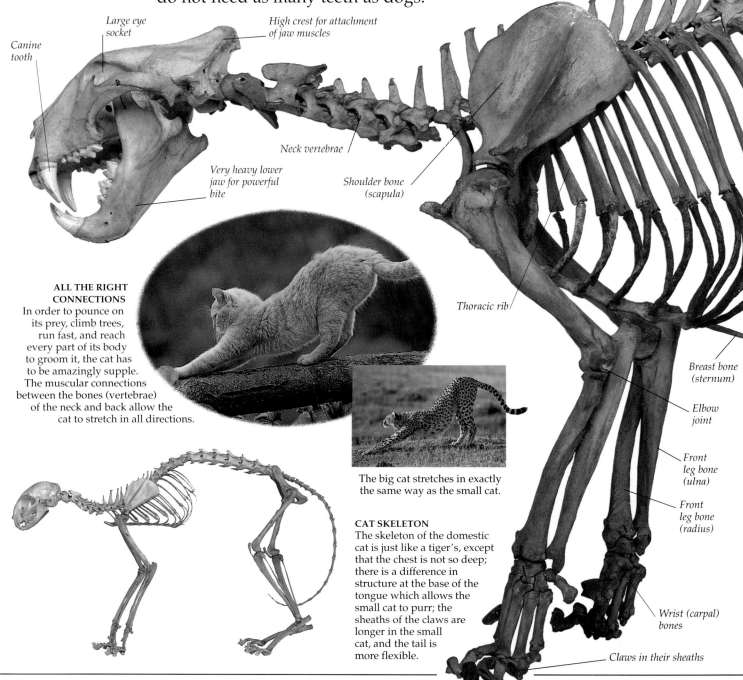

Spine of thoracic vertebrae

Large eye socket

High crest for attachment of jaw muscles

Canine tooth

Neck vertebrae

Very heavy lower jaw for powerful bite

Shoulder bone (scapula)

ALL THE RIGHT CONNECTIONS
In order to pounce on its prey, climb trees, run fast, and reach every part of its body to groom it, the cat has to be amazingly supple. The muscular connections between the bones (vertebrae) of the neck and back allow the cat to stretch in all directions.

Thoracic rib

The big cat stretches in exactly the same way as the small cat.

CAT SKELETON
The skeleton of the domestic cat is just like a tiger's, except that the chest is not so deep; there is a difference in structure at the base of the tongue which allows the small cat to purr; the sheaths of the claws are longer in the small cat, and the tail is more flexible.

Breast bone (sternum)

Elbow joint

Front leg bone (ulna)

Front leg bone (radius)

Wrist (carpal) bones

Claws in their sheaths

CAT SKULLS

This skull shows the big, round eye sockets of the domestic cat, its short face, and large, sharp teeth. In some breeds of domestic cat, like the Persian, the face has been bred to be so short, that there is hardly any room for the teeth, and the animal snuffles because it cannot breathe properly through its flattened nose.

Eye socket (orbit)

Biting tooth (incisor)

Front view of domestic cat skull

Side view of domestic cat skull

Killing tooth (canine)

Cutting tooth (carnassial)

Tiger skeleton

Sacral vertebrae

Lumbar vertebrae

Four false ribs are not attached to the sternum

Hip bone (pelvis)

Costal cartilages join the ribs to the sternum

Thigh bone (femur)

Hip joint

Knee cap (patella)

Caudal vertebrae

TIGER SKELETON

The skeletons of all cats are very similar. The skull is rounded with short jaws and a largish brain case (cranium). There are seven neck vertebrae as in all mammals, but they are compressed so that the cat has a rather short neck in comparison to the rest of its body. The rib cage is deep and the powerful hind leg bones are longer than the foreleg bones. The number of bones in the tail varies from species to species; the tiger, for example, has more bones in its tail than the bobcat.

Knee joint

Back leg bone (fibula)

Back leg bone (tibia)

JUST A BITE

This lioness can break a bone with one bite of her strong jaws. All cats can open their mouths very wide. This is due to the thick bones at the angle of the jaw, and the powerful ligaments which join the lower jaw to the upper jaw in a hinge, just below the front of the ear.

The skeleton shows that with so few tail (coccygeal) vertebrae this Manx cat would have had no visible tail

MISSING LINK

Although Manx cats did not originate in the Isle of Man in the Irish Sea, they have been known there for at least 200 years (pp. 58–59). Their lack of a full tail is thought to be due to inbreeding (breeding repeatedly within a closely related group) in the past.

TOEING THE LINE

It is impossible for a person to stand on tip-toe without support; ballet dancers always have blocked toes in their shoes. The joints and bones of all cats' feet have evolved in such a way that they always walk on their toes.

Heel bone (calcaneum)

Hind foot (tarsal) bones

Inside out

Everything about the cat has evolved so that it can feed on other live animals. It has to be a fast thinker, a fast killer, and, in order to outwit other predators, a fast eater. Therefore, all cats have to be very agile and have very fast reactions, so their bodies have to be both thin and powerful. Cats are very intelligent and their brains are large in relation to the size of their bodies. Their diet of meat alone means that both the large and small intestines are relatively short and simple because they don't have to digest vegetable matter. After a kill, the wild cat will gorge itself on the flesh of its prey, and then may go for several days digesting this meat, before it needs to hunt again. The rough tongue can scrape flesh from bones as well as drawing food into the mouth (pp. 20–21). Cats have sweat glands, but their fur covering leaves only those on the paw pads, and in some cases, the nose, effective for heat loss. The male cat has large anal glands which produce the pungent smell that makes most people prefer to have their tom cats neutered.

GENE MACHINE
The curly coat of this rex is an abnormality caused by genetic mutation. Inbreeding reduces gene variability and leads to the appearance of abnormal genes in the offspring.

FLEHMEN
The special grimace (flehmen) of this lion shows that he is using the Jacobson's (taste-smell) organ to tell if there is a lioness on heat nearby (pp. 16–17). By lifting his head and curling back his upper lip, the lion is drawing the scent-laden air over the Jacobson's organ in the roof of his mouth.

Rounded head with short face

Lithe body

Fur

A fur coat has many uses. It keeps the cat warm, acts as camouflage, carries the scent of the animal, and by means of the sensitive roots of each hair, it acts as an organ of touch (pp. 16–17). All wild cats have a two-layered coat. First, there is an undercoat of fine soft wool, and this is covered by an outer coat of coarser, longer hairs (guard hairs). The hairs of this top coat carry the coat's spotted or striped pattern.

Whiskers

SPOT ME
The spotted coat of the leopard is a perfect camouflage and makes it invisible in the sun-dappled, wooded grasslands where it lives. Only the tawny-yellow eyes of this leopard would be seen staring intently and waiting for any movement that might mean the possibility of a meal.

FUR COATS
It is easy to see how very different the furs of cats are when they are placed side by side in this way. It is also easy to see why, for hundreds of years, they have been used as fur coats for humans. Today, people realize that it is cruel to kill animals for their furs.

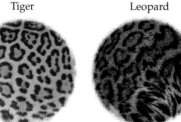

Tiger   Leopard   Panther

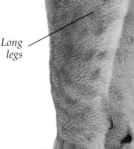

Jaguar   Ocelot   Serval

Long legs

Claws

Claws are formed of keratin, a protein which also forms the outer layer of skin, and is found in human nails. The cat's hind paws have four claws, the fore paws have five. The fifth claw is placed rather like a thumb and helps the cat to grip when climbing or holding prey.

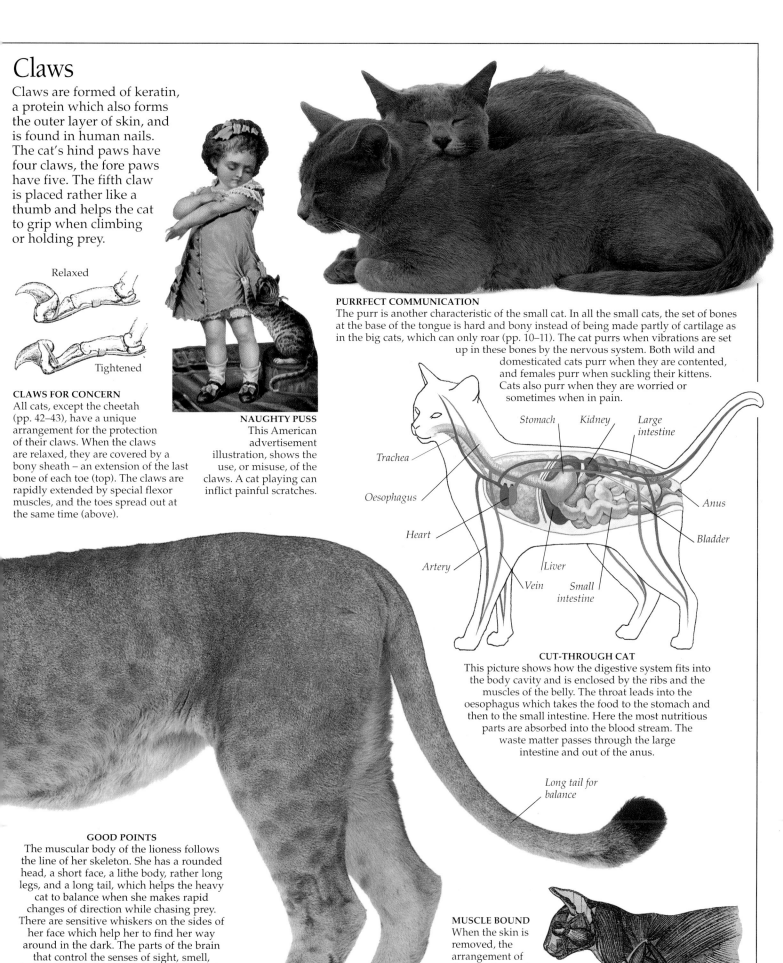

Relaxed

Tightened

CLAWS FOR CONCERN
All cats, except the cheetah (pp. 42–43), have a unique arrangement for the protection of their claws. When the claws are relaxed, they are covered by a bony sheath – an extension of the last bone of each toe (top). The claws are rapidly extended by special flexor muscles, and the toes spread out at the same time (above).

NAUGHTY PUSS
This American advertisement illustration, shows the use, or misuse, of the claws. A cat playing can inflict painful scratches.

PURRFECT COMMUNICATION
The purr is another characteristic of the small cat. In all the small cats, the set of bones at the base of the tongue is hard and bony instead of being made partly of cartilage as in the big cats, which can only roar (pp. 10–11). The cat purrs when vibrations are set up in these bones by the nervous system. Both wild and domesticated cats purr when they are contented, and females purr when suckling their kittens. Cats also purr when they are worried or sometimes when in pain.

Stomach   Kidney   Large intestine

Trachea

Oesophagus

Anus

Heart

Bladder

Artery

Liver

Vein   Small intestine

CUT-THROUGH CAT
This picture shows how the digestive system fits into the body cavity and is enclosed by the ribs and the muscles of the belly. The throat leads into the oesophagus which takes the food to the stomach and then to the small intestine. Here the most nutritious parts are absorbed into the blood stream. The waste matter passes through the large intestine and out of the anus.

Long tail for balance

GOOD POINTS
The muscular body of the lioness follows the line of her skeleton. She has a rounded head, a short face, a lithe body, rather long legs, and a long tail, which helps the heavy cat to balance when she makes rapid changes of direction while chasing prey. There are sensitive whiskers on the sides of her face which help her to find her way around in the dark. The parts of the brain that control the senses of sight, smell, hearing, and balance are particularly well-developed in all cats, both big and small.

MUSCLE BOUND
When the skin is removed, the arrangement of the muscles can be seen. The muscles of the shoulder are very powerful and are used when the cat leaps onto its prey.

Supersenses

MIND THE GAP
Cats are able to judge distances and spaces very accurately. As well as the whiskers, the guard (outer) hairs are also highly sensitive to the minutest pressure. So if there is room for the fur, there is room for the cat inside.

TIME FOR A DRINK
A puma drinks from a freshwater pool. All cats except the sand cat (pp. 38–39) need water regularly, and can taste it in a way that people cannot.

Most WILD CATS LIVE on their own and hunt for food at night. Because of this, they have very highly developed senses, so that they can move quietly, see everything around them, hear the slightest noise, and smell any other animal that is near them in the dark. The small cat kills quickly and usually eats as fast as possible, because it must always be on the alert, prepared to rush up a tree or dive down a hole if danger threatens. Cats have one sense that humans do not have – the "taste-smell" sense – which amongst other things, enables the male to know when the female is on heat (pp. 14–15). The homing instinct of cats is legendary and there are countless stories of cats finding their way home over long distances. This may be due partly to their highly developed senses, but they may have other ways of knowing where they are which we do not fully understand. One theory is that they use a strong magnetic sense.

Pupils expanded (*above*), narrowed (*below*)

THE EYES HAVE IT
A cat can see about six times better than a human at night because it has a layer of extra reflecting cells in its eyes (the *tapetum lucidum*) which absorb light. These reflectors shine in the dark when a cat's eyes are caught in the glare of a headlight.

PUPIL POWER
The eyes of a cat are large in relation to its face. They are quite round and look forwards as well as in a wide angle all around the head. In darkness, the pupils expand to enormous size in order to allow as much light as possible to enter. In bright light, they narrow to tiny slits in the small cats and to tighter circles in most of the big cats.

CELL MATES
In 1601, the Earl of Southampton was imprisoned in the Tower of London, for his part in a rebellion against Elizabeth I. The story goes that his cat, living in the Earl's London house, found its way alone across the city to the Tower. Once there, he crossed roofs and battlements until he found the room in which the Earl was imprisoned. But how to get in? The clever cat somehow located the chamber's chimney, and climbed down to join his owner. This triumphant tale of feline navigational skills may well be true, because this painting was done at the time.

STRETCH 'N' SNIFF
When cats are presented with food or come across any strange object, they are always cautious. They may first reach out and gently tap it with a paw, before stretching out and exploring further with the nose.

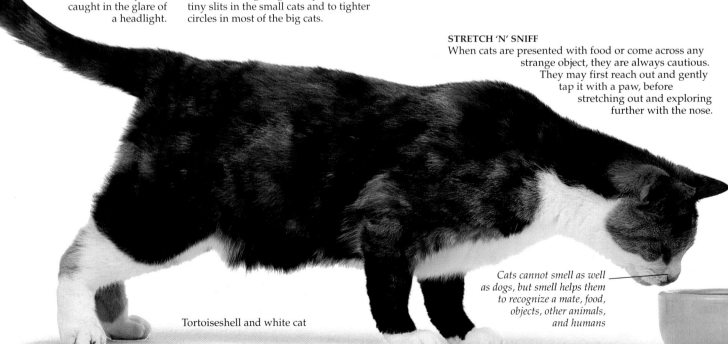

Tortoiseshell and white cat

Cats cannot smell as well as dogs, but smell helps them to recognize a mate, food, objects, other animals, and humans

FIVE SENSES

In all the cats, the five senses of sight, hearing, smell, taste, and touch are more highly developed than they are in humans. Although humans are more sensitive to colour, cats make better use of the light. When it is too dark for even a cat to see, it can still hear prey or danger and successfully feel its way about with its whiskers, its feet, and the very sensitive outer (guard) hairs of its body and tail fur.

Large, funnel-shaped ears draw sound waves into the inner ear, so that the cat can judge the direction of a noise

Eyes open wide when a cat is alert and interested and close to a slit when it is angry and frightened

THE CAT'S WHISKERS

Whiskers are long, stiff hairs with sensitive nerve endings at their roots. They spread out round the face of the cat so that it can feel where it is in relation to objects nearby. In bad light, they act as a back up to the cat's sight.

Thc nose, which has no fur covering, is a very sensitive organ. It draws in scents to receptors on many thin, curled bones in the front of the skull

Rough tongue used for grooming the coat, cleaning kittens, and lapping up liquids (pp. 20–21). Sense of taste is important, because as the cat bolts its meat, it must be able to distinguish quickly any part that might be rotten and harmful

Sorrel Abyssinian

Magnificent movers

EVERY PART OF THE CAT'S BODY is adapted for instant action and perfectly balanced movement. All cats, even the heaviest, like the lion and the tiger, are extremely agile and can leap with great power, although, apart from the cheetah (pp. 42–43), they cannot run very fast over any distance. Their agility and strength is essential, because all cats kill their prey by stalking and then pouncing onto the animal's back and biting its neck. The muscles and bones of the chest and neck are particularly powerful (pp.14–15), and the ligaments very flexible. Unlike many other carnivores, the cat has collar bones, which prevent it from jarring its shoulders when it leaps from a height. The shoulder blades are placed well on the side of the deep chest (pp. 12–13), which helps the cat to climb, and most of the weight is carried on the forelimbs. Cats that climb trees, like the leopard (pp. 32–33), have long tails which help them to balance. All cats walk on their toes (pp. 12–13) and their feet have thick, soft pads so they can move quietly.

WILD CAT STRIKE
A big cat is so powerful that it can kill with one lunge of a paw. This lion knows its strength and would never hurt another member of its pride.

Cat is at full stretch in mid-leap

Cat puts all four paws together for maximum power at take-off

ONE GIANT LEAP...
All cats can jump, and like other animals they do this by flexing and relaxing the muscles of the limbs and the back, while at the same time balancing with the tail. Where the cat differs from other jumping animals, is that it is able to pinpoint its landing position with great accuracy. This is a necessity for a hunter of fast-moving, small prey.

Cat balances on back paws as it begins leap

Puma cub

NINE LIVES
Cats can fall from great heights and always seem to land on their feet. Many of the small cats, as well as the leopard, spend a great part of their lives in trees. Their marvellous sense of balance is an adaptation to the difficult task of hunting a fast-moving animal, such as a squirrel, or a bird, whilst creeping along a flimsy branch. The nervous system has evolved so that the cat, even in the midst of a fall, can right itself so as not to damage its head or the soft parts of its body when it reaches ground. There is a lot of truth in the old saying that "a cat has nine lives" because, by its fast reactions, it can escape from situations that would kill other animals.

When running slowly, opposite legs go together. Right front leg and left hind leg move in unison

PRACTICE MAKES PERFECT
All cubs and kittens have to exercise their limbs and body muscles before they can achieve the flexibility and agile movements of their parents. This young cub's paws seem to be too big for its body, but it is practising running and stalking and will soon be as lithe as its mother.

RUNNING WILD

When a cat runs fast, it pushes off with both back legs at the same time to achieve a maximum forward movement, but places the front paws down separately, although in quick succession. This famous sequence by Eadweard Muybridge was taken in 1887, and clearly shows how a cat moves its limbs when running.

Front paws land and cat begins to bring back paws forward

All four paws touch land

Tail is essential for balance like the pole carried by a tightrope walker

COOL CAT

All cats can probably swim if they have to but few seem to enjoy it. The tiger is an exception. A good swimmer, it spends a fair amount of time in or near water. Tigers living in the tropical rain forests of Asia use water as a means of keeping cool.

Loose skin, and muscles not yet developed

UP A GUM TREE

All kittens have to learn to climb. At first, just like children, they are frightened of falling and are not good judges of their own capabilities. Kittens often venture too far up a tree or onto a roof and are then terrified of going on or back. After a few misadventures and false starts, however, all but the most timid take the plunge earthwards and land on their feet.

BALANCING ACT

This cat shows how it can walk along the top of a very high, very narrow fence without concern. It places its paws neatly one in front of the other and is never in danger of falling.

Cleaning up

THE CAT IS AN EXCEPTIONALLY CLEAN ANIMAL. All cats, big, small, wild, and domestic, spend a great deal of time licking their fur with their rough tongues, pulling bits of dirt out of their feet, and wiping their faces with their paws. When a cat has cleaned itself it is always ready for anything, from instant sleep to fast action. Grooming spreads the cat's own scent from glands under its skin, over its entire body and onto objects which it rubs against. It also acts as a method of calming and "relaxing" the cat. It is not known why domestic cats bury their own faeces, but it is a most convenient habit as far as their human owners are concerned. Many wild cats, like the tiger, do not do this, but deposit their excreta in a prominent position to mark their territory with its smell. Although it is the cleanliness itself that seems to us to be all important to the cat, from the cat's viewpoint, the licking, rubbing, "sharpening of claws", and depositing of excreta in fixed spots (pp. 26–27), is all part of a complex pattern of communication through smell and touch.

Most cats are not fond of water, but these kittens on a beach by famous cat artist Louis Wain (1860–1939) are having a good time

Flexibility of neck allows cat to reach all parts of the body

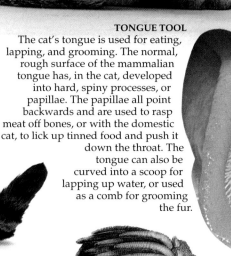

TONGUE TOOL
The cat's tongue is used for eating, lapping, and grooming. The normal, rough surface of the mammalian tongue has, in the cat, developed into hard, spiny processes, or papillae. The papillae all point backwards and are used to rasp meat off bones, or with the domestic cat, to lick up tinned food and push it down the throat. The tongue can also be curved into a scoop for lapping up water, or used as a comb for grooming the fur.

BELLY BRUSH UP
By licking its chest and belly, the cat is cleaning its fur and getting it to lie straight and comfortably. But this licking also strengthens the cat's own smell after it has been stroked or has fed its kittens.

Close-up of papillae showing how they all point backwards

Papillae, each shaped like a miniature tongue

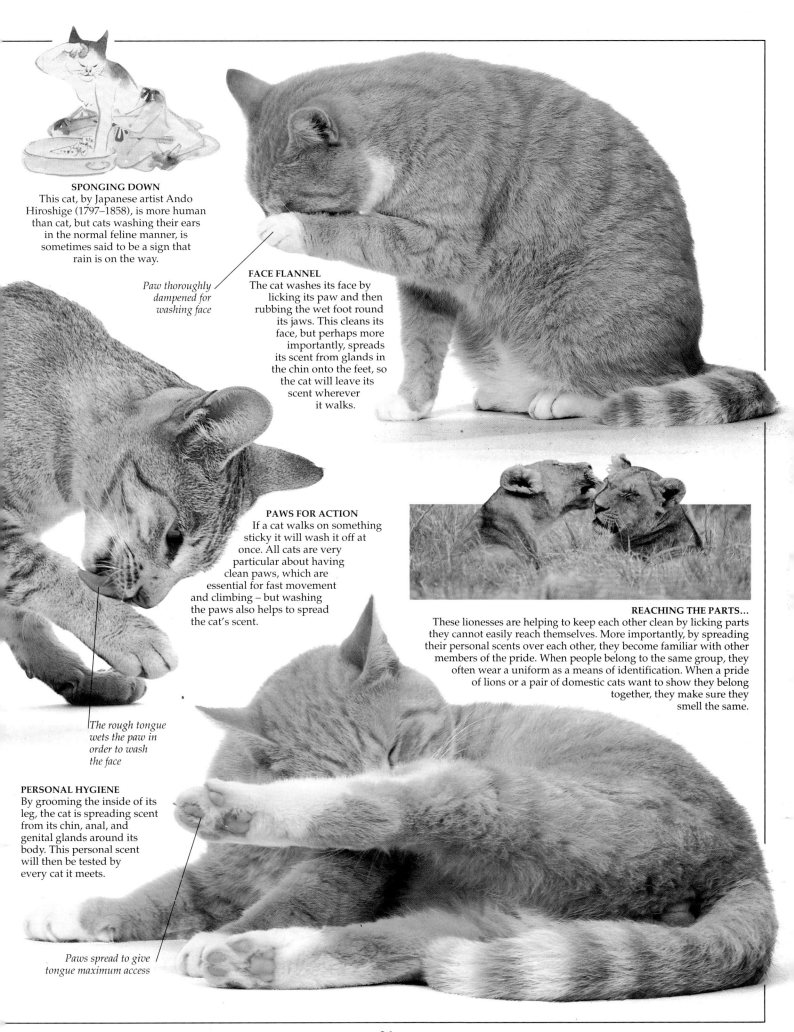

SPONGING DOWN
This cat, by Japanese artist Ando Hiroshige (1797–1858), is more human than cat, but cats washing their ears in the normal feline manner, is sometimes said to be a sign that rain is on the way.

Paw thoroughly dampened for washing face

FACE FLANNEL
The cat washes its face by licking its paw and then rubbing the wet foot round its jaws. This cleans its face, but perhaps more importantly, spreads its scent from glands in the chin onto the feet, so the cat will leave its scent wherever it walks.

PAWS FOR ACTION
If a cat walks on something sticky it will wash it off at once. All cats are very particular about having clean paws, which are essential for fast movement and climbing – but washing the paws also helps to spread the cat's scent.

REACHING THE PARTS...
These lionesses are helping to keep each other clean by licking parts they cannot easily reach themselves. More importantly, by spreading their personal scents over each other, they become familiar with other members of the pride. When people belong to the same group, they often wear a uniform as a means of identification. When a pride of lions or a pair of domestic cats want to show they belong together, they make sure they smell the same.

The rough tongue wets the paw in order to wash the face

PERSONAL HYGIENE
By grooming the inside of its leg, the cat is spreading scent from its chin, anal, and genital glands around its body. This personal scent will then be tested by every cat it meets.

Paws spread to give tongue maximum access

Playing cat and mouse

TOM AND JERRY
In the famous cartoon, quickwitted mouse Jerry often gets the better of the swashbuckling, but slightly stupid Tom – not often the case in real life.

IN THE WILD, all cats feed on the flesh of the animals they have killed. Cats are solitary hunters, except for the lion which hunts in a family group (pride, pp. 28–29). Cats usually kill animals smaller than themselves, although occasionally they will attack a larger animal. Motionless animals sometimes escape attack, but with practice, cats can recognize prey by sound and scent alone. They have an excellent memory for places and will return many times to a spot where they once had successful hunting. Cats stalk their prey, sometimes for a long time, then with a sudden rush, leap on it and sink their sharp canine teeth into the neck. Small cats feed mostly on mice, birds, lizards, beetles, and any other small animals they can catch. Large cats, like the leopard, feed on bigger animals about the size of a goat, and often drag their prey up into trees to keep it away from other predators. Male domestic cats that play with prey, are probably keeping their kittenish behaviour into adult life in the protected world of the human home.

A stalking cat holds its body close to the ground

The pads on a cat's paws help it to move silently

READY FOR ACTION
This black leopard (also known as a panther) is stalking, and getting ready for the kill. Every part of the body is alerted. A cat on the prowl moves very slowly and silently until it is near enough to make a quick and decisive pounce. All cats hunt in this way, from a lion killing a buffalo, to a domestic cat killing a house mouse.

MEDIEVAL MOUSERS
This medieval picture comes from a 13th-century book called *The Harleian Bestiary*. It is interesting because it is such an early illustration of cats with a rat, although the cats are not at all realistically painted.

IN FOR THE KILL
Cats very often choose a vantage point from which they can see but not be seen. This cat would have sat absolutely silently and still on the fence for some time, watching the happenings in the grass below, before leaping down with great accuracy on the unsuspecting prey.

Black panther

A FISHY BUSINESS
The fishing cat of India does not hunt for its food
quite like any other cat. It can flip fish out of the
water with its slightly webbed paws, and
several times has been seen diving for fish
which it catches in its mouth.

TELLING TAILS
The cat's tail is a
barometer of its moods.
It lashes it when angry
and twitches it gently to and fro
when concentrating or contented.

RUNNING DOWN
The cheetah and the
springboks are keeping a wary
eye on each other. The cheetah will
not begin to hunt unless there is an
antelope on its own in a vulnerable position.
The antelopes know this and they will not be
disturbed unless the cheetah comes too close.
However, once the prey has been singled out,
the cheetah will pursue it at great speed.

A PRACTISED KILLER
Many cats, both wild and domestic, play with their prey before
killing it. Mother cats teach their kittens how to hunt by
capturing prey, and releasing it, to allow the kittens
to watch their actions. It is not really known why
adult cats with no kittens still play with their
prey. It may be that some cats keep their
kittenish behaviour in adult life.

*A cat playing with
a toy is reacting as
if it were prey*

Serval

CHICKEN DINNER
This serval, like the other
small cats, crouches down
to eat its food. When big cats
eat, they tend to lie down with
the food positioned between
their front paws. Small cats
begin by eating the head,
which is swallowed whole
with very little chewing.

BIG MEAL
With its massive teeth, this tiger can
snap a bone with one bite, and will
devour a whole carcass, skin and all.

The young ones

Leopard with cubs in their den

T<small>HE YOUNG OF THE LARGE CATS</small> are usually called cubs while the young of the small cats are called kittens. All cats, whether large or small, are tiny, helpless babies when they are born, and are blind until they are at least nine days old. There are usually about four kittens in a litter, and the mother looks after them on her own with no help from the father cat. Cats need a secure place in which to give birth. Domestic cats usually select a safe, dark spot like a drawer or cupboard. In the wild, most members of the cat family, from the bobcat to the tiger, give birth in a den. Kittens take around 63 days to develop (gestate) in the mother's womb, and after birth the mother suckles them for six to eight weeks before they are weaned and begin to eat meat. They are fully independent at about six months, but many young cats stay with their mothers for up to two years. The gestation period of cubs, like the lion cub, is between 100 and 119 days. When they are born, they are very small compared to the size of the mother, and they are not weaned until they are three months old.

KNITTING KITTEN
The kitten in this Japanese scroll is happily playing with a ball of wool. "Toys" play an important part standing in for prey, and allowing kittens to practise catching and hunting techniques.

FAMILY GATHERING
Although domestic cats like these may live in a town flat and have no contact with life in the wild, they still have all the instincts of wild cats. These kittens are now too old to suckle, but the mother continues to protect and groom them. She also teaches them how to clean themselves and where to excrete. Cats taken away from their mothers too soon, grow into neurotic and disturbed adults, as can happen with orphaned human children.

THE COURT OF THE KING
When a lioness comes on heat and is ready to mate, the chief lion in a pride stays close to her and prevents other lions approaching. He mates with her many times over the two or three days that she is receptive to him. Each time takes only a few seconds.

Kitten grows adult coat of fine hairs over its woolly undercoat

MOGGIES MATING
A female cat only allows a male to mate with her when she is on heat. In domestic cats, this usually happens twice a year. Each mating takes only a few seconds but may occur several times with different males in the three to five days that the female is on heat (pp. 60–61).

IDENTITY CRISIS
Cubs and kittens often
have differently marked
coats from the adults. This
spotty baby is, in fact, a puma.
Its spots merge into stripes
and it has a ringed tail. These
slowly fade as the cub grows
up. Lion cubs also often have
spots which fade as they
mature. In some domestic
breeds, such as the Siamese, the
kittens are born pale all over.
The dark points only develop
as the cat becomes adult.

PLAYING ABOUT
Play is an essential part of growing-up. It teaches the
young animal how to kill its prey and how to "get on"
with its fellows. These kittens have to learn how to
fight, but they must learn when to stop as well, so
they are not badly hurt. Play also exercises the
muscles of young animals and helps the brain
and nervous system to develop quick reactions.

Sorrel
Abyssinian
cat and kittens

*Mother's rough tongue grooms
kitten, helping it to understand
about other cats' scents*

*Legs are
slightly bandy
and uncertain
at first*

CUB CARRIAGE
All mother cats are expert at carrying their
young from place to place at the first hint
of danger. This lioness has grasped the
loose skin around the neck of her cub
between her teeth and lifts
it off the ground without
hurting it at all.

*Several pairs of teats for suckling – each
kitten has its own teat and uses no other*

Cat characteristics

Engraving of a terrified cat

A LL CATS, WHETHER LARGE OR SMALL, wild or domesticated, behave in very similar ways. The wild cat gives birth in her den, protected from possible predators. The domestic tabby, secure in her house, still seeks a safe, dark place to have her young. Apart from the lion, all cats are solitary hunters, and also eat alone. They are strongly territorial animals, and all mark their territory, whether it is a couple of gardens or a stretch of forest, in the same way – by spraying urine and by depositing excreta. They also exchange scents in the same ways, by rubbing and licking each other. Cats, both large and small, communicate and have various noises in common. Chirruping a greeting and yowling are two with which everyone is familiar. All cats sleep a great deal, mostly in the day, so that they are ready for the activities of the night. Even domestic cats will follow this pattern of behaviour, and do not adapt their timekeeping to suit their human owners, except where feeding times are concerned. Unlike dogs, cats can rarely be trained; they have adjusted to living with humans, but have never changed their essential character.

LION LINGO
Ever since the evolution of our human ancestors several million years ago, the roar of the lion has been the most frightening of all animal sounds. However, the lion roars as a means of communicating with the rest of the pride, rather than to frighten its prey.

CAT NAP
Cats sleep a great deal. In some hot countries, they may sleep, in all, as much as 18 hours a day, hunting and feeding in the cooler hours. Cats do not usually sleep in long stretches but in a series of shortish periods. They often have one eye partly open, on the look out for any danger.

FRIEND...
Cats value their personal space. This cat feels hers is threatened and that the other cat has come too close, so she has crouched down low in a defensive position. Sometimes cats erect all their hairs so that they appear enormous.

Flattened ears are a warning sign

Hissing indicates that this cat does not want to be interfered with and will fight if she has to

PUTTING OUR HEADS TOGETHER
Cats which live together, like domestic cats or lions, sometimes rub each other's heads to show that they have no intention of fighting. Young cats do this more often, especially when they are excited.

LEGGINGS
Cats often rub against people's legs. It shows affection and also extends the cat's personal scent onto the human.

LEAVING A MESSAGE
All cats mark their territory with urine and secretions from their glands. This is called spraying and they all do it in the same way. The cat backs up to a post or tree, lifts its rump high and, with the tail held straight up, discharges a stream of pungent fluid against the object.

SMARTENING UP
Cats spend a good deal of their time "sharpening their claws". This is really stretching their limbs by digging their claws into a wooden tree (or silk-covered sofa!), and pulling the claws downwards. The claws are probably not sharpened by this act, but they are cleaned, and the muscles of the feet and limbs are exercised. Sometimes a houseproud cat-owner will have the cat's claws removed because it is destroying furniture, but this denies the cat one of its most natural activities.

Back slightly arched to make cat look bigger

LIONESS SCRATCHING
Lions can tear the bark off a tree when "sharpening their claws".

CAT CLUB
This illustration of a cat's club from a Victorian children's book presents a delightfully fanciful idea of cats socialising and having a good time. In real life, domestic cat colonies are based on the availability of food supplies, and consist of extended families of closely related females, with perhaps a few dominant males attached.

...OR FOE?
Cats test each other's reactions with an explorative paw. This cat is seeing how near he can go to the tortoiseshell cat. Because he is getting a very negative reaction he will probably stalk off, pretending to be more interested in something else.

Twitching tail shows that the cat is in an excited state

ROLY POLY
Both large and small cats roll over on their backs to show affection. They only expose their bellies in this way when they feel totally secure. Rolling is often done by female cats when they are coming into heat (pp. 24–25).

Top cat

PERSIAN PLATE
This delightful plate from Iran shows a lion standing with the sun rising behind him. This was the symbol of Iranian kingship.

MORE THAN 10,000 years ago, when all humans were living as hunter-gatherers, there were lions living over the whole of Europe and Asia as well as in Africa. The lions competed with humans for the same prey and gained the respect from their human rivals which exists to the present day. Apart from a small population in the Gir forest in northwest India, lions today are found only in Africa. They live in family groups, or prides, of up to 12 animals and help each other to hunt. Because of their family support, they are the only cats which are able to kill animals larger than themselves. The role of the male lions is to defend their territory. They do this by pacing around it, by roaring, and by marking trees and posts with their urine (pp. 26–27). The females (lionesses) do most of the hunting. Each lioness will give birth every two years to about five cubs. If a new lion takes over a pride, he may kill any cubs the lionesses have before he mates with them.

THE KING
His magnificent mane, heavy body, and huge canine teeth ensure that the lion rules his world. Although lionesses are the hunters of a pride, the male lions are given prime place at a kill and are allowed to feed first.

African lion and lioness

The lioness has no mane as it would impede her efficiency as a hunter

THE PRIDE
The composition of a pride varies, but females always outnumber males. When a young male reaches adulthood, the resident male usually drives him away from the pride. The young male will seek out and attach himself to a group of females in need of a male. A pride of lions shares its territory with many other meat eaters, competing for every scrap of meat left over when the pride has had its fill.

MATE TO KING
The lionesses are the core of any pride, sticking together with close family – sisters, daughters, and aunts. The lioness has a powerful, lithe body so she can creep stealthily up to prey, before moving in for the kill.

LEO
People born under the astrological sign of Leo are said to be proud, brave, strong, and self-centred – just like the king of beasts himself.

DANIEL IN THE LIONS' DEN
In the Old Testament, Daniel, a high-born Jewish man, was taken to the court of Babylonian King Nebuchadnezzar as a captive. He was able to interpret several of the king's dreams and rose to a powerful position, but was overthrown and cast into the lions' den. Because God was on his side, the lions did him no harm.

THE LION AND THE UNICORN
In the Renaissance (the 15th and 16th centuries) the lion often appeared in paintings and architecture. In this beautiful French tapestry, the lion is shown to be at peace with the unicorn, symbol of purity.

HERACLES AND THE NEMEAN LION
Heracles had to perform 12 labours to pay for the killing of his family. The first was to kill the lion whose skin could not be pierced by weapons, so Heracles choked it to death. After this, he wore the skin to protect himself.

The mane makes the lion look even bigger than he really is. It may help to frighten off other lions

The tuft of hair at the knees makes the lion look even stronger

The still visible spots are a leftover from when the lioness was a cub

The tuft at the end of the tail is an important signal in communication

Tiger, tiger, burning bright

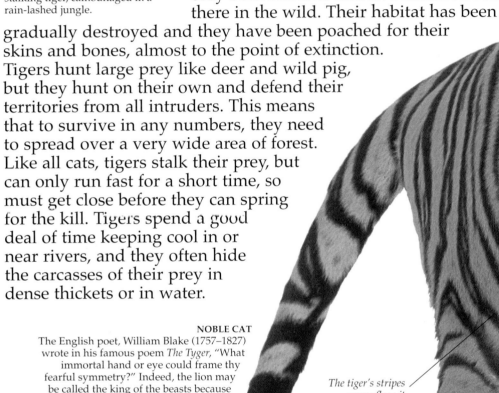

STORM TIGER
In this famous picture, painted by French artist Henri Rousseau (1844–1910), it is hard to see the stalking tiger, camouflaged in a rain-lashed jungle.

Tigers are the biggest and most powerful of all cats. They used to live, in small numbers, in many of the forests of India, Southeast Asia, and through China as far north as Siberia. Today, this magnificent animal is an endangered species clinging on to survival in a few tropical forest reserves, and in swamps, like those of the the Ganges delta in India. The biggest of all tigers come from the snow-covered forests of Siberia, but there are only between four and five hundred still living there in the wild. Their habitat has been gradually destroyed and they have been poached for their skins and bones, almost to the point of extinction. Tigers hunt large prey like deer and wild pig, but they hunt on their own and defend their territories from all intruders. This means that to survive in any numbers, they need to spread over a very wide area of forest. Like all cats, tigers stalk their prey, but can only run fast for a short time, so must get close before they can spring for the kill. Tigers spend a good deal of time keeping cool in or near rivers, and they often hide the carcasses of their prey in dense thickets or in water.

NOBLE CAT
The English poet, William Blake (1757–1827) wrote in his famous poem *The Tyger*, "What immortal hand or eye could frame thy fearful symmetry?" Indeed, the lion may be called the king of the beasts because of its great mane and proud carriage, but the tiger is more awesome. Although it is so huge, – tigers in India weigh up to 260 kg (573 lb) and the Siberian tiger is even heavier – the tiger lives and hunts in just the same ways as all other cats.

Very long, closely striped tail

MASS MURDER
In India, the tiger was always respected until the coming of the Europeans, who considered slaying the noble beast from the safety of an elephant's back, a good day's "sport". In the mid-19th century, when the British ruled India (the Raj), huge numbers of tigers were slaughtered during shooting parties. In 1888, the British even offered a reward to anyone who killed one. Today, the tiger is again respected, and the Indian government has set up *Project Tiger* to save it from extinction.

The tiger's stripes camouflage it in long grass and forests

Heavy body is close to the ground so the tiger can be hidden in grass or water

ONE TOO MANY?
A mosaic pavement, dating from the first to second century A.D. was discovered in Leadenhall Street, in London, England. It shows the god Bacchus, who was the god of wine, nonchalantly riding a tiger.

TIGER BY A TORRENT
This hanging scroll, painted in 1795 by the Japanese artist, Kishi Ganku (1756–1838), depicts in great detail, a fierce tiger beside a rather more loosely painted raging torrent.

The stripes on the back are more dispersed

Rounded head with long whiskers

Man-eating tigers

Although tigers do not usually kill humans, sometimes they do become man-eaters. Often they are injured by humans, and are no longer able to kill wild animals. Or it may be because people are fishing or working in their territories, scaring away their natural prey. In India, the government is doing everything it can to keep people and tigers apart.

TIPPU'S TIGER
This large mechanical "toy" was made during the latter part of the Mughal empire (1526–1857) in India. When wound by the handle on the side, the tiger attacks the English soldier.

The huge paw is so powerful, that it can knock prey over with one blow

EYES IN THE BACK OF YOUR HEAD
Tigers almost always attack from behind, and in the Sundarbans forest and swamp between India and Bangladesh, it has been found that a face mask worn on the back of the head has stopped tigers from attacking forest workers.

Tree climber

LEOPARDS LIVE IN WOODED GRASSLANDS in Africa and southern Asia, and are the biggest cats to climb trees regularly. Leopards are skilled climbers and climb vertical trunks with complete ease. They are bulkier than cheetahs, but not such heavy animals as lions or tigers. They are secretive animals and stealthy hunters, hunting mostly at night, although they are sometimes seen in daylight hours. Leopards almost always live on their own. They may occasionally prey upon domestic livestock, but also kill animals such as baboons and cane rats which destroy crops. Both males and females defend their territory by spray marking branches and tree trunks with their urine and by seeing off intruders. Cubs are looked after by the mother until they are about two years old when they can fend for themselves. Leopard numbers are under threat everywhere, mainly because of the destruction of habitat, but also because they have very desirable fur coats.

LEAFY LARDER
This lounging leopard has clearly had too much for lunch. Leopards often carry the animals they kill into trees. This protects the carcasses from packs of scavengers like hyenas and jackals, who would soon scrounge the food from the solitary leopard, if it were left on the ground.

Leopards do not often roar but communicate by means of a rasping bark

THE JOURNEY OF THE MAGI
This beautiful Renaissance painting by Gozzoli, was commissioned by Piero de Medici for the chapel of the family palace in Florence, Italy. The young boy sitting in front of the leopard was the Duke of Lucca whose family emblem was the leopard. The Medicis kept these cats for hunting, and there is a leopard on a leash in the foreground.

LEOPARD
The black spots on a tawny-yellow background act as perfect camouflage for this shy animal, when it is hiding in the dappled leaves of a tree or in long, dry grass. As with most animals, the coat is short and sleek in countries where the climate is hot, but becomes much thicker and therefore warmer, in colder climates.

Spotless

The sleek black panther is just a leopard with hidden spots. The black colour comes from a combination of genes which can occur in many other species including the jaguar and the domestic cat. The panther behaves just like spotted leopards and breeds freely with them.

PANTHER
If you look closely you can see the spots on this black panther's coat. This (melanistic) form of leopard coat is most common in the forests of Southeast Asia.

BAGHEERA
Bagheera the black panther, played an important part in the upbringing of Mowgli, the jungle boy from Rudyard Kipling's *The Jungle Book*.

SNOW LEOPARD
This very rare, large cat is not the same species as the true leopard. It lives only in the high mountains of central Asia. Snow leopards are solitary hunters and feed on wild goats, hares, and marmots.

The spots look much better on a leopard than on a fur coat

The leopard's tail is long and darkly ringed

The soft-looking paw hides sharp claws used for killing prey and climbing trees

BENIN BRONZE
This bronze plaque, made in the Bini kingdom in Nigeria in the 16th or 17th century, decorated the king's palace. The leopard was an important animal in Benin myths and was known as the King of the Bush. It was chosen as ruler over the animals for its power, beauty, good nature, and wisdom, and only the king was allowed to kill leopards.

Water cat

THE JAGUAR IS THE ONLY LARGE CAT to be found in the American continents. The name jaguar comes from *yaguara*, its name in the languages of the Amazon peoples. It lives throughout South America, as far south as Patagonia, and until quite recently, jaguars were also fairly common in the southern states of the USA. However, although it is protected today, the jaguar is nevertheless in danger of extinction, because of continued destruction of its forest habitats for development, and because, until recently, thousands upon thousands were killed for their exceptionally beautiful, spotted coats. The jaguar is rather like a leopard, but larger and not as lithe and agile. A solitary hunter, it kills tapirs, sloths, turtles, and other small animals. It can climb trees, but not very well, and prefers to hunt at ground level or in water. A jaguar maintains a territory which varies from 5 to 500 sq km (2 to 200 sq miles), depending on the availability of prey.

JAGUAR
This engraving shows clearly what a sturdy cat the jaguar is.

CAT CULT
The jaguar played an important part in much South American mythology. This pottery vessel from the Inca civilisation in Peru, shows a jaguar eating its victim.

Ringed spots merge to blotches on the belly

Long tail helps the jaguar to balance

GRUNTER HUNTER
The jaguar is not such a bold hunter as the leopard, and is generally slower. Unlike most big cats, it rarely roars. It grunts frequently when hunting and growls when threatened. Jaguars have sometimes been tamed, and occasionally one has even been known to live in a house, like a huge pussy cat!

JAGUAR KNIGHTS
Aztec warriors in Mexico belonged to either the order of the eagles or the jaguars. At the end of the summer, the eagles and the jaguars paraded in an annual military display. As shown here in stylized form in an Aztec book, the *Codex Cospi*, the jaguar knights wore a skin with the head used as a helmet.

AQUACAT
Jaguars are most at home in the dense, tropical forests of South America. Forest jaguars are darker than those living in grasslands. They swim well and have been known to kill crocodiles. The Amazon peoples believe that jaguars lure fish to the surface by twitching their tails in the water and then flip the fish out with their paws. River turtles are a favourite food.

TAPIR TRAPPER
Tapirs look rather like large pigs, and were once an important part of the jaguar's diet. They live in the same thick forests around the Amazon as the jaguar, but today tapirs are very scarce.

Spotted head held low

Reddish-coloured spots. Forest jaguars are darker than those living in grasslands

Short, massively powerful foreleg

The heavy body of the jaguar is a bit like a lion's

TIAHUANACO TAPESTRY
This Peruvian tapestry, made approximately 1,000 years ago, shows the importance of the jaguar in Peruvian society. Here a full-face jaguar head, is flanked by two standing (*rampant*) jaguars.

High society

ELIZABETHAN LYNX
A lynx, illustrated 500
years ago in England.

THE LYNX, BOBCAT, AND PUMA or cougar, are called small cats, although they are not particularly small (the puma is, in fact, the largest of all the small cats). However, their body structure is like the small cats and not like the big cats. The lynx and the bobcat are alike, and different from all other cats, in that they have very short tails. Both cats feed on animals the size of hares, and in Canada, lynx numbers vary from year to year, depending on the population of its main prey, the snowshoe hare. The bobcat lives in North America, the lynx in North America, Europe, and Asia, and the puma in North and South America. Although the lynx is found in forests in Europe, all three are most at home amongst rocky landscapes and high up on mountain slopes, sometimes as much as 4,500 m (15,000 ft) above sea level.

TRAPPED
Hunting for bobcat and lynx is still permitted in North America and some 70,000 bobcats a year are trapped for the fur trade, often in vicious gin traps like this. Many people believe that they should be banned as they have been in Britain for a number of years.

Bobcat cleaning itself, by the great American artist and naturalist, John James Audubon (1785–1851)

Short, stumpy tail

Bobcat

Unlike the lynx, the bobcat has only short tufts on its ears

Thick side-whiskers look rather like a mane

BOBCAT
The spotted coat of the bobcat camouflages it in the rocks and bushy vegetation where it lives. Bobcats are solitary hunters that prey on small animals. They will sunbathe, in fine weather, in places where they feel secure. When mating, they caterwaul like domestic cats, only their screams are louder and more shrill. The female gives birth in a den lined with grass or moss and hidden in rocks.

The puma has a long, furry tail with a black tip, unlike the bobcat and the lynx

The hind legs are longer than the front legs making the puma a good stalker

The puma's coat can vary in colour, but the underside is always pale

LYNX

The lynx is best adapted to life in high pine forests and thick scrub where its unspotted, brownish coat is invisible against moss and rocks. The long tufts on its ears are thought to help the lynx to hear well in dense forests where sound does not carry far. It also has very big feet which, in winter, are covered with thick fur that acts like a snow shoe and prevents the lynx sinking into the snow.

Lynx in summer coat

Lynx in winter coat

PUMA POWER
In the Mochica culture in Peru around 600 B.C., the puma was worshipped as a god. This golden, sacred puma was possibly used for some kind of ritual. It is intricately decorated with rows of double-headed snakes.

PUMA

The puma is an adaptable cat as much at home on the inhospitable, windswept shores at the tip of South America, as on the slopes of the Colorado mountains in the western USA. It hides itself away in rocky places and is a good climber, so is seldom seen, although it hunts by day as well as by night. Pumas have large territories and cover many square kilometres in their hunt for prey.

The pupils are circular, and do not contract to slits as in the smaller cats

Puma

CHANGE OF SCENE
Although the puma is often found in mountainous regions, it can also live in the tropical rain forests of the Amazon.

Plains drifters

MANY CATS LIVE in grasslands (savanna), plains, and even in deserts. The lion is the largest cat that lives in grasslands. Two other good-sized plains cats, the serval and the caracal, are very widespread, ranging over the whole African continent and into western Asia. They are considerably bigger than the rest of the savanna cats. Plains cats are mainly nocturnal, and hunt for small animals like birds, rodents, lizards, beetles, and snakes. They have longer legs than forest cats and are fairly speedy over short distances, as they have to escape from larger predators, such as hyenas, that might kill them for food. The caracal is also called the desert lynx because it has tufts on its ears, but it does not have such a short tail as the northern lynx. The serval has been hunted in East Africa for its meat as well as for its fur – not for the western fur trade but for traditional cloaks, or *carosses*, worn by East Africans.

Black ears with tufts of hair about 4.5 cm (1.75 in) long

CARACAL
Caracal is a Turkish word meaning "black ears". The caracal has a wider distribution than the serval and is found in western Asia and India, as well as in Africa. It usually has a litter of two or three kittens which are born in borrowed burrows, rock holes, or thick scrub. It does not usually make much noise, but has a loud bark which it uses to call its mate.

BIRD BASHER
In India and Persia (now Iran), the caracal, which is easily tamed, was trained to catch hares and birds. It is a supreme bird catcher, and sometimes leaps into the air after birds, which it catches by batting them with a paw. Caracals climb well, and have been known to kill eagles roosting in trees.

Long, strong legs allow bursts of speed

IN UP TO THE NECK
The caracal lives in tall grasslands, dry scrub, and semi-desert. It is found in central India and south-western Asia, as well as Africa.

SERVAL
The serval is one of the most striking of the savanna cats. With its small head, spotted coat, and long legs, the serval looks rather like a small cheetah. It hunts small animals and always prefers to live near water. It is found throughout central and southern Africa and in north-west Africa. The serval climbs well and, like the caracal, often catches birds.

SAND CAT
The rarely seen sand cat is a true desert dweller. It sleeps during the sweltering heat of day in a dune burrow or under scrub. At night, it comes out of its den to hunt small desert animals like lizards and mice. It manages to exist without water, getting sufficient liquid from its prey. The sand cat has thick, furry pads on its feet, so it can move fast over soft sand, and its yellowy-brown coat blends into the desert. Sand cats live in the Sahara and the deserts of western Asia.

Short, ringed tail with dark tip

Very long, front legs built for speed

Short, dense fur keeps the cat warm at night and cool in the day

BLACK-FOOTED CAT
This is the smallest of all wild cats, less than half the size of an African wildcat (pp. 44–45), but it is claimed to be very fierce. So-called because the soles of its feet are black, it lives in open, semi-desert country in southern Africa.

Tail is one-third of the length of the head and body

Forest felines

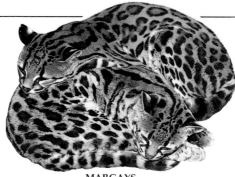

Ocelot

Most of the small cats live in woodlands, forests, or jungles and they range over every continent except Australasia. Forest cats, like all members of the family Felidae except the lion (pp. 28–29), are solitary hunters that kill smaller animals such as mice and lizards. They feed when they can, and will eat pretty much anything that they are able to catch. They are almost all very striking in appearance, with powerful, lithe bodies, spotted or striped fur, and huge eyes to aid night hunting (pp. 16–17). They are extremely shy and hard to see in their habitats, where they are well camouflaged. They are generally silent creatures but the males try to see off their enemies by caterwauling. All the species are in danger of extinction both from increasing loss of habitat and also because, in spite of legal protection and a great deal of international publicity, they are still hunted for their fur, particularly in South America where poverty forces people to earn money any way they can.

MARGAYS
The margay looks like a smaller version of the ocelot, but it is slimmer with longer legs and tail. It feeds on birds and lives in forest trees in South America. Very little is known about it.

LEOPARD CAT
The leopard cat is the most common wild cat of southern Asia. It is about the same size as a domestic cat and also looks quite like one. It is a good climber and an excellent swimmer and has therefore been able to colonize small offshore islands. In China, they are known as money cats because the spots look like small coins.

NOT A LOTTA OCELOT!
Although mainly a forest cat, the ocelot is also to be found in grass and scrubland from Arizona to Argentina. Ocelots often live in pairs, hunt by day, and swim well. Forest ocelots have a darker coat than those that live in scrub. In Mexico, because of the stripes around its neck, it is known as "tigrillo" or "little tiger". It is the most frequently hunted small cat in South America.

FLAT-HEADED CAT
This is a rare and elusive cat from India and parts of Southeast Asia. It has dark brown fur tipped with white which gives it a silvery appearance. Little is known about its behaviour, but it appears to live along river banks, probably catching fish, frogs, and birds, as well as small mammals.

Spots at the base of the tail become rings at the tip

Ocelot

Geoffroy's cat

The white ear spots are used to signal to other cats

GEOFFROY'S CAT
Geoffroy's cat (called after its discoverer, Etienne Geoffroy St. Hilaire, a 19th-century French naturalist) lives in forests and jungles from Patagonia to Bolivia in South America. It can live at high altitudes and in Argentina is known as "the mountain cat". It swims and climbs well and often sleeps in trees during the daylight hours.

The dark spots are similar but smaller than those of the ocelot

The claws, hidden by the soft pads, are sharpened by climbing

CUTTING BACK
If deforestation (destruction of the forests and jungles) for development continues at the present rate, the delicate balance of nature will be overturned for ever and the beautiful cats that live in the forests will soon become extinct.

Speed king

THE CHEETAH IS THE FASTEST LAND ANIMAL in the world. It has a short head and a beautiful fur coat like the other cats, but in some ways it hardly seems like a true cat. Unlike other cats which are all leaping cats (pp. 10–11), the cheetah can be called a running cat because it has evolved to hunt fast-running animals, such as the gazelle, in open country. For this reason it is placed in a different group from all other cats and given a different Latin name, *Acinonyx jubatus*. The cheetah selects its prey by stalking in the usual way, but then, at very high speed, it will chase after the gazelle or antelope and kill it with a sharp bite into the neck. It will also eat hares and guinea fowl, and very occasionally even ostriches. Female cheetahs live alone and guard their territories, only allowing visiting males to come near when they come on heat (pp. 24–25). Unlike the solitary females, male cheetahs may often live together in a small group, but only the dominant male will mate with a female. The male group will not allow any other males into their territory and have even been known to kill intruders.

Small head with short, rounded ears

FAST FORWARD
The long legs and flexible backbone of the cheetah enable it to run at up to 96 kmh (60 mph), faster than any other land animal. Film has shown that the cheetah can reach its maximum speed in three seconds, from a standing start.

NO CONTEST
The acceleration of a cheetah is comparable to this powerful Ferrari, although the animal can only keep up its speed for about 170 m (550 ft). Car drivers should *never* try to race cheetahs.

Slender, long legs

Narrow, dog-like paws

NO COVER UP
Like the dog, the cheetah needs to have extended claws when it is running, to help it to get a good grip on the ground. So, unlike all other cats, the cheetah does not have a protective sheath over each claw. The claws are fairly blunt, only slightly curved, and very strong.

WANDERING WAYS

The mother cheetah usually gives birth to between one and eight cubs which are hidden in long grass while they are very young. She does not have a permanent den but moves her cubs around every few days.

Supple, muscular back

Powerful hindquarters

INDIAN TAKE-AWAY

In the past, cheetahs were often caught and trained to help huntsmen kill antelope and gazelle. Indian miniatures, painted to record the reign of the Mughal emperor Akbar in the 16th century, show the cheetahs' role. They were sent after prey, and having knocked it down would wait for their owners to complete the kill and take the carcass away.

CHEETAH

Cheetahs are becoming very rare. In wildlife parks their daytime activities are frequently disturbed by tourists, and, although protected by law, they are still killed by poachers for their fur. Cheetahs used to be found throughout Africa and across into India, but today the main population lives in Namibia and Zimbabwe. The cheetah hunts by day and usually drags its kill into bushes so that it cannot be driven off its meal by vultures and other carnivores.

ALL FURRED UP

The fur on the neck and the shoulders is thicker than elsewhere. It forms a sort of "mane", which is hardly visible in adults, but shows clearly, as in this Victorian engraving, in cubs and in young animals.

The striped tail is more than half the length of the head and body

MERGER

The king cheetah of Zimbabwe and southern Africa, is a very rare variety, and was once classed as a separate species. The spots on its coat join up to form stripes on its back.

Cats' kin

Broader head and longer face than a domestic cat's

ALL THE MANY DIFFERENT BREEDS of domestic cat that are found in the world today, from Europe to Japan, are descended from one wild species called in Latin *Felis silvestris*, the wildcat. This small cat is a very widespread and highly adaptable species, which explains why it has found it so easy and comfortable to live closely with humans. The wildcat lives in the forests of Europe, the rocky lands of western Asia and India, and the grasslands of Africa, and differs slightly in each habitat. In northern Europe, the wildcat (*Felis silvestris grampia*) has a stocky body and thick fur, to cope with life in cold climates. In Africa, where the climate is hot, the cat (*Felis silvestris lybica*) has a finer body, longer legs, and short hair. In India, the wildcat or Indian desert cat (*Felis silvestris ornata*) lives in hot, dry country, and is usually spotted. The wildcat shows many slight colour variations, and the female is usually paler than the male. The wildcat from Africa is most likely to be the ancestor of the domestic cat, which was called by Linnaeus, *Felis catus* (pp. 10–11).

WILD IN THE HIGHLANDS
This Scottish wildcat is still found in small numbers in the forests of Scotland, but it is in danger of extinction, because it interbreeds with domestic cats which are living wild (feral cats pp. 60–61). This cat is like a large, heavily built tabby, but it is much fiercer.

Scottish wildcat

Shortish tail with blunt end

WEE WILDCATS
Kittens usually go out hunting with their mother at about 12 weeks and are independent at about five months. Although kittens of the African wildcat can become good pets, Scottish wildcat kittens have proved difficult to tame.

OUT OF AFRICA
African wildcats live all over Africa in many different habitats from deserts to woodlands. When mating, they caterwaul like domestic cats and also miaow harshly. They are not as shy as northern wildcats and often live close to villages and farms, interbreeding with domestic cats.

NOT CHOOSY
The Indian desert cat will interbreed with the northern wildcat, the African wildcat, and the domestic cat, so it certainly could have played a part in the ancestry of the domestic cat. It has a long, black-tipped tail and the soles of its feet are black. It lives in hot, dry places and hunts small animals such as mice and lizards.

Ragged ears probably indicate many battles

CATS RULE, OK?
The domestic tabby is not very different from its wild ancestor in its looks and behaviour. Indeed, it has been said that the cat has tamed people and not the other way around (pp. 26–27).

Close relatives
The civet and the genet are not true cats although they are sometimes mistaken for them and behave like them. They are carnivores, and belong to the mongoose family which also includes the rare linsangs and the meerkat. Although on the outside their heads are similar to those of cats, the skulls are different.

GENET
Although this little animal has a long, very un-catlike tail, its head looks similar to a cat's.

CIVET
The civet and the genet are both forest dwellers and hunt and feed at night. Their bodies are patterned with spots or stripes.

Indian desert (or wild) cat

The taming of the cat

CATS PROBABLY BEGAN LIVING NEAR HUMAN SETTLEMENTS because it was easy to catch the rats and mice that were feeding on stored grain. People soon saw how useful cats were at destroying these pests, so they were encouraged to remain. Any kittens born nearby would have been tamed and soon the cat was part of the household. Nobody knows when cats first started living with people, but it was probably at least 5,000 years ago. At the height of the great Egyptian civilization 3,000 years ago, the cat was already a common domestic animal, and it appears in many Egyptian tomb paintings. Eventually, the cat became one of the most sacred animals in Egypt. It is, therefore, probable that the cat was first domesticated by the ancient Egyptians, and that the wildcat of North Africa is the most likely ancestor of all domestic cats (pp. 44–45). However, it is also possible that the cat was tamed at about the same time in many different countries of Europe and Asia, wherever the wildcat lived. Today, there are domestic cats in every part of the world where there are humans.

MUMMIFIED MOGGY
When one of the sacred cats of ancient Egypt died, its body was mummified (treated to prevent decay), wrapped in bandages, and placed in a special tomb. When archaeologists began to excavate these tombs during the last century, they found millions of mummified cats piled on top of each other.

PERSIAN PUSS
The fluffy, longhaired cats from Persia (now Iran) belong to one of the oldest breeds of domestic cat, although this ancient, hollow earthenware model, painted with lustre, from the 13th century, looks more like a spotted cat than the longhaired breed (pp. 56–57). Most longhaired pedigree cats throughout the world today, are descended from cats brought from Turkey and Iran in the 18th and 19th centuries.

Egyptian mau

ANCIENT IMAGE
The spotted Egyptian mau is a domestic cat originating in Egypt. "Mau" is the ancient Egyptian word for cat. Although this is a new breed which first appeared in Europe in the 1950s, its graceful, lithe body, green eyes, and the pale background colour of the coat, make it more like the cats of ancient Egypt than perhaps any other cat, with the possible exception of the Abyssinian (pp. 52–53).

POMPEIAN PET
After the volcanic eruption of Mount Vesuvius in Italy in A.D. 79, nearby Pompeii and Herculaneum were destroyed, but the lava which covered the towns preserved a lot of evidence of the life there. This mosaic of a cat carrying off a bird was found in almost perfect condition.

FIGHTING LIKE CAT AND DOG
Two Greek men appear to be encouraging their animals to fight. It is interesting to see that both the cat and the dog are on leads. The way the dog is standing, with its front legs squatting and its nose pushed forward, shows that it doesn't really want to fight. It just wants to tease the cat which is arching its back ready to attack.

CATCHER CAT
A wall painting in the tomb of an Egyptian sculptor, Nebamun, (around 1400 B.C.), is a scene of the dead man catching wildfowl in the Nile delta. This detail shows his cat holding two birds in its claws and one in its mouth, assisting its owner by retrieving the birds.

CAT ON A PEDESTAL
Cat adoration in Egypt reached a peak with worship of the cat goddess Bast, usually shown as a woman with a cat's head. She often carried a sistrum (a musical instrument) and an aegis (a shield) decorated with a lioness's head. She was associated with happiness and warmth, and loved people dancing and having a good time.

Because cats were considered sacred, they were often used to decorate jewellery, like this Egyptian gold and cornelian ring.

SLAYING THE SERPENT
In this illustration from the Egyptian *Book of the Dead*, the sun god Ra, in the form of a cat, slays Apep, the serpent of darkness.

Myths and legends

FOR THE LAST 3,000 YEARS, since they were first treated as sacred animals by the ancient Egyptians, cats have played a major role in the folklore of many countries all over the world. Dogs have never achieved the same prominence in stories and legends. This may be because cats are such enigmatic creatures: in the daytime they are often soft, sleepy, and affectionate, but at night they turn into silent and efficient hunters. In many European countries, huge numbers of cats were cruelly killed in the late Middle Ages, because they were thought to be associated with witchcraft. On the whole, they had a much better time in eastern countries such as Myanmar (Burma), where any magical powers were thought to be for the good. At sea too, they enjoyed a good reputation, not only because they killed rats on board ship, but also because many sailors believed that they could forecast storms.

COMRADE CAT
Cats often play a prominent part in Russian fairy tales.

HAUNTING TALE
In the West, traditionally, cats do not have ghosts. But in Japan, cats have the power to turn into super-spirits when they die. This may be because in the Buddhist religion, the body of the cat is the temporary resting place of the soul of very spiritual people.

BLESSED BIRMAN
The Birman is the sacred cat of Myanmar. According to legend, a Burmese temple was attacked and the high priest killed. His favourite white temple cat jumped onto his head and was transformed into a Birman. Where the paws touched the priest, the fur remained white, a symbol of goodness. This miracle encouraged the remaining priests to repel the invaders.

CAT CHARIOT
During the early Renaissance period in Europe, the cat was widely persecuted. This was perhaps because of a revival of interest in the Norse love goddess Freya, whose chariot was drawn by cats. This spurred the Christian church to attempt to purge Europe of the symbols of paganism.

FAMILIAR CATS
From about 1400, for about 300 years the cat was thought of as a witch's "familiar", her private connection with the devil. Witches were also thought to be able to turn themselves into cats at will. Many cats were therefore persecuted, and there were mass burnings in many parts of Europe, most notably in Metz in northern France.

BOND CAT
Ernst Blofeld, the arch-enemy of 007 spy James Bond, when confronting James, always had a white Persian cat at his side.

PUSS-IN-BOOTS
In southern France, there was once a wide belief in *matagots* or magician cats. One of the most famous of these was Puss-in-Boots, created by Charles Perrault. This cat was so crafty, that it won for its master a fortune, and a princess for a wife.

British black shorthair

BLACK MAGIC
Belief as to whether a black cat brings good or bad luck, has varied over the centuries, and from country to country. In Britain, a black cat crossing your path brings good luck, while in some states in the American mid-West, it is good luck if a black cat visits your house, but bad luck if it stays.

Aristocats

IN THE MID-19TH CENTURY it became fashionable to own exotic cats, and clubs were formed to determine standards and compare types. During the 20th century, the fashions of the show ring led to many breeds being developed that look amazingly different from the wild ancestor of every cat, and it is difficult to remember that inside every champion there is a wild animal with the instincts of a hunter. But the basic behavioural patterns of the cats do not change, although they may appear to do so. Sometimes, this is because the kittens of pedigree cats are reared in a cattery in large numbers, for sale, and not individually in a human home. If a cat is to be an affectionate companion, it must be handled and talked to from as soon after birth as possible. If it is brought up without this sort of human contact, and then taken from its mother at six weeks old to be placed with a family, it may appear neurotic. This is often put down to its highly bred or aristocratic temperament whereas, in fact, it is due to lack of social contact from birth and from being removed from its mother too soon.

FIRST SHOW
Harrison Weir, who staged the world's first modern cat show in London in 1871, is seen with the winner, a Persian kitten.

SHOW OFF
It is argued that the showing of pedigree cats has helped to create the great variety of breeds in the world today, although many people find experimentation in breeding distasteful. This champion Birman certainly does not look unhappy with the luxurious trappings of success.

FIT AND FLUFFED-UP
Grooming longhaired cats is important at all times (pp. 62–63) to prevent tangling, and to get rid of excess hair. It is particularly important before a cat show, when a cat should look fluffed-up and in peak condition.

ORANGES
Red self longhairs were originally known, for obvious reasons, as oranges. This is a fairly rare breed. The beautiful red coat should show no shading or tabby markings.

Deep orange coat

Thick-set, cobby body

Ears are sometimes almost transparent

Body is muscular but elegant

The Russian blue has a very "aristocratic" profile. The nose is wedge-shaped and the ears are large and slightly pointed

Russian blue

Wide-set, almost turquoise eyes

BLUE BEAUTY
The Russian blue has had a great many names in its history including Spanish cat and Maltese cat, but it is generally thought to be a Russian breed. Certainly, the breed was exported to Britain in the 16th century. One of the most famous was Vashka, the beloved pet of Tsar Nicholas I.

Long, fine - boned legs with small, oval paws

Thick, plush double coat, stands out from the cat's body because of its density

Long, tapering tail

Powerful hind legs

Large, round, copper-coloured eyes

Red self longhair

Small, rounded ears

UNLUCKY THIRTEEN
In 1898, a party of 13 dined at London's famous Savoy Hotel. The first guest to leave was killed soon after, fulfilling an old superstition. In the 1920s, sculptor Basil Ionides was commissioned to carve a wooden cat about 1 m (3 ft) high. At the Savoy today, Kaspar the cat always sits at table when there are 13 diners, and is served the whole meal.

The red self has a very different profile from the Russian blue. The nose is so flat that the animal sometimes has trouble breathing through it

Short, solid legs

51

Shorthairs

Almost all cats had short hair until about 100 years ago. This was because the cat could survive and fend for itself more easily if its coat was short. There was no danger of it becoming tangled in branches, or of enemies grabbing it, and less chance of a skin disease as a result of matted fur. Even today, the shorthaired breeds are more robust. Pedigree shorthaired cats fall into three main categories: the British shorthair, the American shorthair, and the foreign or Oriental shorthair. The British shorthair is a stocky, muscular cat with shortish legs. The American shorthair developed from ancestors of the British shorthairs which were taken to the USA by early settlers. It is larger and more lithe than the British type and has slightly longer legs. In Australia too, cats arrived with the first settlers in about 1788. Among the most popular cats today are the Oriental shorthairs. These are sleeker than the other shorthairs with smaller heads and longer legs. The Siamese and Abyssinian are two well-known breeds. There are many non-pedigree shorthaired cats, of all shapes and sizes, and these cats can be as beautiful as their pure-bred cousins.

American portraits, like this one by Ammi Phillips (1788–1865), often included the family pet

Large, pointed ears set far apart

Almond-shaped green eyes

SEW MUCH FUN
In the early part of the 20th century, cutely painted kittens, like the two here, were often used to illustrate birthday cards and postcards. Cotton reels are still favourite playthings for kittens.

ABYSSINIAN
No-one knows for sure where the Abyssinian was first bred, but it looks like the cats shown on ancient Egyptian tomb paintings. It comes in many colours including usual (brown), sorrel (light copper), blue, fawn, lilac (pinkish-grey), and silver. It is a beautiful and very graceful cat.

Small, oval-shaped paws with black pads

Longish tail tipped with black

*Large ears set
high on the head*

*Heart-shaped face
with very round,
bright green eyes*

*Tortoiseshell-and-
white coat covers
thick-set body*

TORTOISESHELL-AND-WHITE
These pretty cats, with their distinctive coats, are
very familiar but are very hard to breed. To produce a
tortoiseshell, females are best mated to a solid-coloured black,
red, or cream male, but even then there may be only one or no
kittens with the desired colouring. Tortoiseshells are almost
always females. They are cats of great character and make
charming family pets.

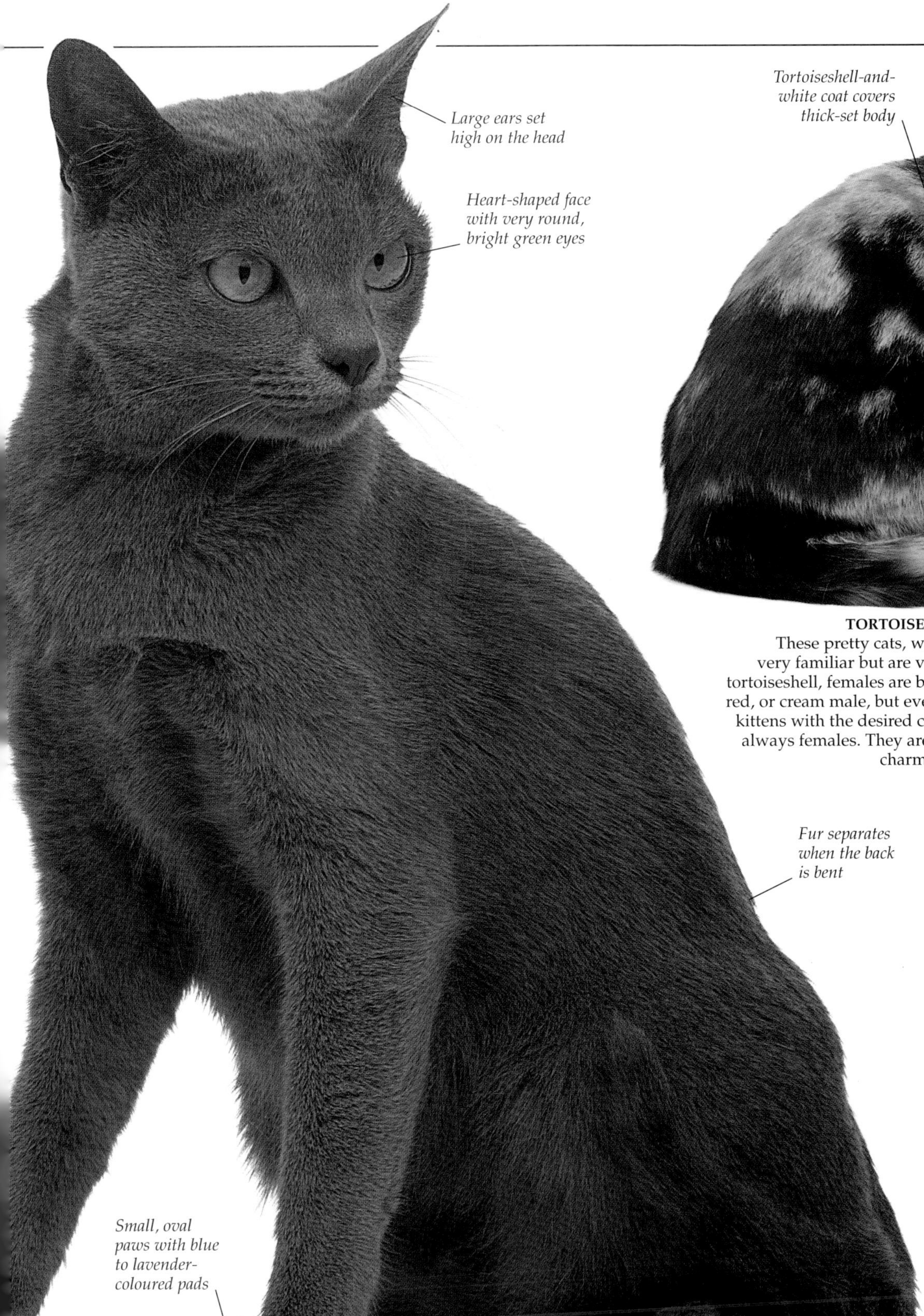

*Fur separates
when the back
is bent*

LOOK-OUT
Like all cats, this tabby likes to
know what's going on and has
selected a good perch. Non-
pedigree cats are sometimes less
nervous than highly bred cats
(pp. 50–51) and usually make
good pets.

*Small, oval
paws with blue
to lavender-
coloured pads*

KORAT
The korat is one of the oldest breeds
of cat. It comes originally from
Thailand, and is thought to bring
good luck to its owner. The breed was
first taken to the USA in the 1950s, but
did not arrive in Britain until the
1970s. It is a gentle, rather nervous
cat. It has a heart-shaped head and a
dusky blue coat, and is little changed
from its ancient ancestor.

BURMESE
Like the Abyssinian, the Burmese
comes in a variety of coat colours, of
which brown is the original, and to
some, the ideal colour. Brown cats,
similar to today's Burmese, were
recorded as living in Buddhist
temples in Myanmar as long ago as
the 15th century. It is an affectionate,
intelligent cat that hates to be left
alone, and loves to lie on beds.

Continued on next page

MR AND MRS CLARK AND PERCY
There is no doubt that artists like painting cats. From the time of Leonardo da Vinci to the present day, cats have appeared in great works of art. In this famous painting by David Hockney of his friend Ossie Clark and Ossie's ex-wife Celia Birtwell, their large white cat is almost the centre of the painting.

HOPE SPRINGS ETERNAL
This cat can smell that there has been a bird in the cage.

Ginger and white cat

MR. MISTOFFELEES
Old Possum's Book of Practical Cats by T. S. Eliot describes wonderful cats, full of character. Mr. Mistoffelees (like all black cats pp. 48–49) has his own share of magic. Indeed, Eliot describes him as "The Original Conjuring Cat".

Ringed, fluffy tail

MISS ZOE DE BELLECOURT
This very proper 18th-century girl was painted by the Scottish artist George Watson (1767–1837). Cats were considered to be most suitable pets for young ladies at this time.

COLOUR CHANGE
Because of the popularity of the Russian blue, attempts have been made to produce all-black and all-white versions of it. For some reason, Russian blues are most popular in New Zealand.

BEATEN BY A HEAD
This extremely unusual piece of American naive art showing a cat head with a bird in its mouth, was perhaps painted as a tribute to a good hunting cat (cats played an important part in early American homesteads), or may have been someone's family emblem.

SIAMESE
Cats similar to the Siamese lived in Thailand (formerly Siam), for hundreds of years. The first Siamese to arrive in Britain in the 1880s are believed to have been a gift to the British consul from the Court of Siam. It is a highly intelligent, noisy cat, and very often will not tolerate rivals for its owner's affections.

Thin, tapering tail .

Long, pointed ears

Tabby cat

Fluffy coat in excellent condition

Bright eyes are a sign of health

TWO'S COMPANY
More non-pedigree cats have tabby coats than any other kind of markings. Non-pedigree cats are often more robust than highly bred cats, because inbreeding (pp. 12–13) can cause physical weaknesses. These two cats clearly "get on". They display no aggressive signs to each other.

Long, slim legs

Small, neat paws

Longhairs

Famous French artist, author, and cat-lover Jean Cocteau (1889–1963), designed this logo

ALL WILD CATS HAVE A TWO-LAYER FUR COAT (pp. 14–15), and in cold countries, all mammals, including cats, tend to have thicker and longer fur than those from hot countries. But no wild cat has the luxurious fur of the longhaired domestic cat (although Pallas's cat comes near to it). Long hair would be a disadvantage to a wild cat because it would become matted and tangled in bushes (pp. 52–53). However, because longhaired cats are very attractive, this characteristic was specially selected by cat breeders in the past and is now common. The Persian is probably the oldest breed of longhaired cat, and most longhairs are of this type. The breed may have been brought into Europe from western Asia on several occasions over the last few hundred years. Another very old breed is the Angora which came from Turkey. Longhaired cats are usually placid by nature and make excellent animal companions, but they do need more attention than shorthaired cats.

BIRMAN
The Birman, has a longer body than a typical longhair, and markings reminiscent of a Siamese. Although legend has it that the breed evolved from a white temple cat (pp. 48–49), it may, in fact, be a cross between a Siamese and a Persian. It always has white feet.

ANGORA
This early engraving shows an Angora, possibly the first longhair to be seen in Europe. It came originally from Turkey.

Large, round white paws

Neck ruff

Short head with long, pink - tipped nose

TURKISH VANS
This cat is often referred to as the Turkish swimming cat, because it is said to be particularly fond of playing in water. It takes its name from the isolated area around Lake Van in southeast Turkey, where it has been bred for several hundred years.

Long, feathery tail

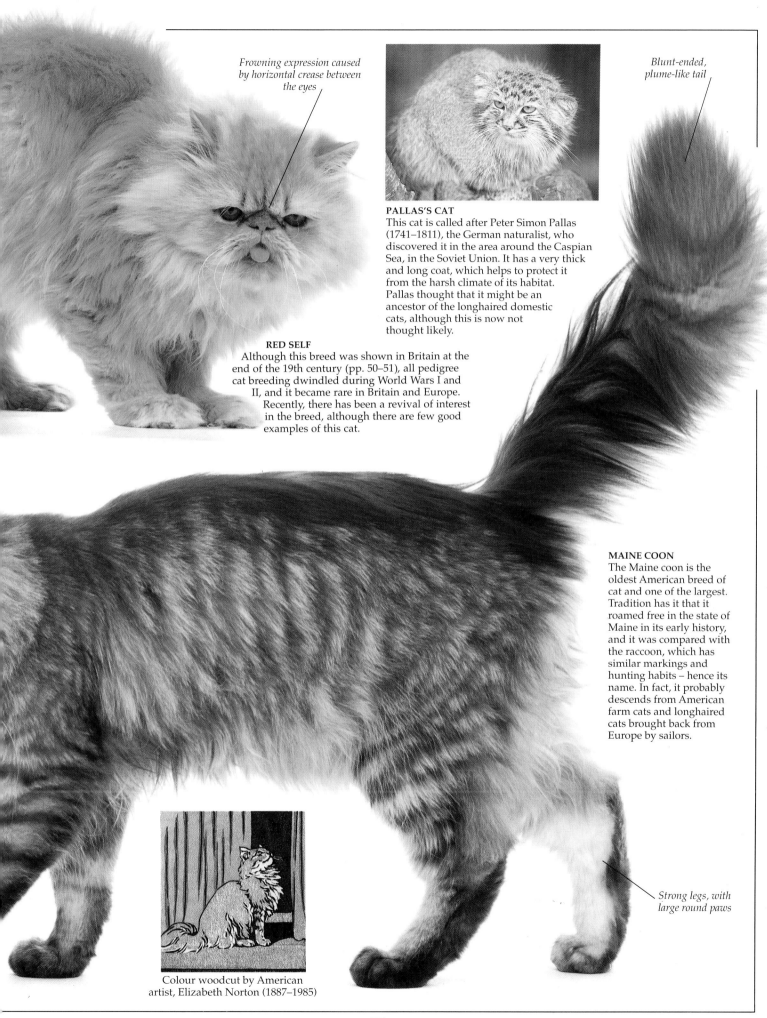

Frowning expression caused by horizontal crease between the eyes

PALLAS'S CAT
This cat is called after Peter Simon Pallas (1741–1811), the German naturalist, who discovered it in the area around the Caspian Sea, in the Soviet Union. It has a very thick and long coat, which helps to protect it from the harsh climate of its habitat. Pallas thought that it might be an ancestor of the longhaired domestic cats, although this is now not thought likely.

Blunt-ended, plume-like tail

RED SELF
Although this breed was shown in Britain at the end of the 19th century (pp. 50–51), all pedigree cat breeding dwindled during World Wars I and II, and it became rare in Britain and Europe. Recently, there has been a revival of interest in the breed, although there are few good examples of this cat.

MAINE COON
The Maine coon is the oldest American breed of cat and one of the largest. Tradition has it that it roamed free in the state of Maine in its early history, and it was compared with the raccoon, which has similar markings and hunting habits – hence its name. In fact, it probably descends from American farm cats and longhaired cats brought back from Europe by sailors.

Strong legs, with large round paws

Colour woodcut by American artist, Elizabeth Norton (1887–1985)

CHESHIRE CAT
This stained glass window commemorates the British writer Lewis Carroll (1832–1898) who, in *Alice's Adventures in Wonderland*, immortalized the perpetually grinning Cheshire Cat.

Curious cats

THE BREEDING OF CATS for special characteristics, like different coloured coats, extra big ears, a reduced tail, or very fluffy fur, was only begun at the start of the 20th century (pp. 50–51). In this short time, many different breeds have been developed. By selective breeding, almost any part of the cat can be altered. It is possible that these special features could appear as natural mutations in a wild cat, but the animal would probably die before passing on these abnormalities. In domestication, all sorts of changes can be produced by inbreeding and selection, and offspring can be given very special care, so that the line can be carried on. Sometimes curiosities in the wild, like the white tiger, are perfectly healthy, as are some new domestic breeds like the Burmilla, a cross between a Burmese and a chinchilla. But, all too often, excessive inbreeding produces an animal with serious health problems. Whether breeders should continue trying to develop new breeds is an open question.

THE SPHYNX
The appearance of this cat is certainly not everyone's idea of beauty. Hairless kittens are born from time to time as a natural genetic abnormality. One such kitten, born in 1966 to an ordinary black and white cat in Canada, was used as a founding sire (male cat used for fathering kittens) for a new breed of hairless cats.

DEVON REX
As a result of a mutation, which was selected for the founding of a new breed, the Devon and Cornish (originating from Devon and Cornwall) rex cats are unique in that every hair on their bodies is soft and curly. They are healthy animals and make affectionate family cats.

The curly fur is short, soft, and close-lying with no guard hairs (pp. 14–15)

Devon rex

The head is wedge-shaped with a longish nose. The nose should be roughly the same colour as the coat. The ears are large and slightly rounded, and the eyes are almond-shaped

Even the whiskers are curly

THE OWL AND THE PUSSY CAT
A cat and bird friendship would be a very curious thing indeed. However, in Edward Lear's (1812–1888) famous poem, the owl and the pussy cat are in love, marry, and live happily ever after.

MIX 'N MATCH
In zoos and circuses, lions and tigers sometimes mate. When the father is a lion, the cubs are called ligers, and when the tiger is the father, they are called tigons. These animals although healthy, are often infertile. However, a female liger in Munich was successfully mated back to a lion and the cub reared to adulthood.

Long, flexible tail

MANX
A kitten without a tail may be born in any litter, and the Manx has long been established as a breed. Manx means from the Isle of Man off the northwest coast of England. Although not originally from the island, probably as a result of its geographical isolation, and the resulting inbreeding (pp. 12–13), tailless cats became common there at least 200 years ago.

Well-defined patches of black, cream, orange, and white fur

Manx cats can have no tail at all (a rumpy), have a tiny bump (a riser), a moveable tail stump (a stumpy or stubby), or a small tail (a longy)

Strong back legs

IN BLACK AND WHITE
The striking white tiger was once not uncommon in north and east central India, although there are few there now. The unusual colour is the result of a dominance of white genes similar to those in white domestic cats.

NEATLY FOLDED
Ears that turn over or hang down are a common feature of domestic dogs but are rarely seen in cats, although the folded ear, like absence of a tail, can occur as a natural mutation. A white kitten born in Scotland with folded ears in 1961, was used as a sire for the new breed called the Scottish fold.

Street life

ALL CITIES HAVE A SECRET WORLD of teeming animal life, where hunters and hunted co-exist successfully. Cats find plenty of pigeons, rats, mice, and cockroaches to prey upon in city alleys and drains, and in restaurant dustbins. It is undoubtedly true that some cats are as happy roaming the streets at night looking out for scraps of discarded fish or a live mouse scuttling along a gutter, as they are sitting by a fire being stroked by a human hand. Cats that live in a city have their own territories. They crawl into basements, under sheds and warehouses, or up onto roofs. Male city (alley) cats mark and defend their territories in the same way as pet cats and wild cats. Females also have territories, and will find hidden places to have their kittens. Cats are useful in cities because they clear up debris and get rid of rats and mice. Once, most companies and warehouses kept a cat on the premises for this purpose, but now, preventative poisons are used instead. Urban cats can become too numerous when well-meaning people feed them, and this upsets the balance of the concrete jungle. In some cities, cats are caught, neutered, and released to carry on living their own lives, but they will not breed again.

CATS ON A HOT TIN ROOF
Their roaming natures often mean that cats take to the roof-tops. This territory gives them independence from human interference and probably sometimes allows them access to interesting places. This delightful scene by French artist and engraver, Grandville (1803–1847), is entitled *The heartaches of an English cat.*

The coat is slightly matted, a sign that this cat is not in peak condition

Tabby markings form the basic feline coat pattern

TABBY TEMPERAMENT
It may seem strange, but a cat's temperament is connected to the colour and markings of its coat. Cats that live in cities have to be calm by nature. Blotched tabby cats and black and white cats have the best temperaments for city life.

STREET FIGHTERS
In the USA, there may be as many as 58 million cats and in Britain probably over 4 million. It is not easy to tell the difference between cats that live with people and go out onto the streets at night, and those that live like wild animals, away from human contact the whole time. Street cats are usually rather nervous and scruffy. They run away when approached, and may be grubby with torn ears and sore places from frequent battles.

The ear is ragged and scarred, a certain sign of battles fought

The eye is damaged, either the result of a fight or because of an inadequate diet

TOM, DICK, OR HARRY?
When the female cat is on heat (pp. 24–25), several males in succession may mate with her. This can result in there being more than one father of the kittens in a litter, and they can all look very different, as in the painting above. Indeed, one female is known to have given birth to a very mixed litter of non-pedigree cats and one perfect Siamese.

Feral cats

Feral refers to domestic animals that no longer live under human control, but have returned to live and breed in the wild. Some alley cats living in cities have become feral. Feral cats are often found on islands where they were left by sailors, but where there are now very few humans. These cats can do serious damage to local wildlife.

ONLY A WHISKER
There is a fine line between a street alley cat and a feral cat. Indeed, some people claim that they are one and the same. Certainly, some alley cats can live totally outside human control, but most do depend indirectly on human life.

CATASTROPHE
This Parisian group is protesting against a proposed plan to destroy the feral cat populations living in Paris. The objectors believed that such a move would be a disaster, and upset the natural ecological balance, not only in Paris, but eventually in all France.

Caring for your cat

CATS ARE TRUE INDIVIDUALS with their own needs. The contented fireside cat may change into a solitary hunter once darkness falls, for the domesticated cat always retains wildness in its nature. If possible, every cat should be allowed outside to explore and establish its territory and also to eat the blades of grass that help its digestion. Magnetic cat flaps allow cats maximum freedom and the owners minimum annoyance, as the flap is opened by a magnet on the collar, thus preventing unwelcome visits from other cats. Most people like to get their cat neutered unless they are intending to breed from it. Your vet can tell you the correct age for this. It is also wise to get your cat vaccinated against feline enteritis and cat 'flu. Both can be killers. Kittens are irresistible, but before getting one, you should remember that a cat can live for over 20 years, and will need constant care and attention for all of that time – but the rewards will be great.

Kittens and puppies often appeared on Victorian cards

KAT KIT
All cats, but especially the longhaired breeds, should be brushed regularly, otherwise they swallow a lot of hair when they lick their coats. This collects in the stomach as a fur-ball, which can make the cat ill.

Water bowl

MOGGY MENU
Cats are carnivores and need to eat meat or fish daily. Hard cat biscuits are also a good idea as they help to keep the teeth and jaws clean and healthy. Water should always be available and is essential if dried food is part of the diet. Although cats like milk, it often gives them an upset stomach.

SCRATCH CLEAN
Every cat needs to clean its claws and stretch its body (pp. 26–27). An old piece of wood or mat, or a scratching post, are ideal for this.

Scoop

Food bowl

Gravel or commercial cat litter

Litter tray

CREATURE COMFORTS
The cat is a territorial animal and needs its own sleeping place. However, the cat will often take over the best armchair or bed. This is probably because these places smell reassuring rather than because they are especially comfortable.

DIGGING IN
Nearly all cats can be trained to use a litter tray. The cat carefully buries its excreta, but the tray needs to be cleaned out at least daily, and the litter replaced.

PLAYTIME

Cats love to play and they need the exercise. A ball of screwed-up paper is often enough to distract them. No toy should have any loose string attached, that could wind round the animal's body or strangle it.

COLLARED

Many people think that a cat should not wear a collar because it might get caught on a twig or branch of a tree. However, collars with an elastic strip in them allow the cat to escape in an emergency. In large towns, it is advisable to have one with an identification disc attached.

Front grill can be securely fastened

ON THE ROAD

Cats hate to be taken away from their own territory. They are extremely alert, and most cats know when their owners are about to go on holiday. It is often better to leave them in their own home with someone coming in to feed them, but if this is not possible, or even for the annual visit to the vet, a secure travelling basket with a favourite blanket in it, is important. It should be brought out well in advance of the trip so that the animal can get used to it.

BASKET CASE

Few cats will sleep in a specially provided basket if it does not smell right. Cats like somewhere that smells of their owner. So a cat basket should first be lined with newspaper, to help prevent draughts, and then covered with an old jersey or any other article of clothing, for the "security blanket". All places where the cat sleeps should be kept free from fleas by regular spraying or washing with an insecticide which will not harm the animal.

ALL YOU NEED IS LOVE

The cat not only needs clean food and a warm bed, it also needs affection. In return, it will display love for its owner. Cat ownership has been shown to benefit humans, particularly the old and lonely. The cat provides companionship, and stroking and petting it helps to release frustration and tension.

Did you know?

AMAZING FACTS

A cat's nose pad

A cat's nose pad is ridged with a unique pattern, just like the fingerprint of a human.

There are more than 500 million domestic cats in the world.

A cat's heart beats nearly twice as fast as a human heart, at 110 to 140 beats per minute.

For a cat, the grass is red! Cats are partially colour blind, so that red colours appear green and green colours appear red.

In just seven years, a single pair of cats and their offspring could produce a staggering total of 420,000 kittens.

Sir Isaac Newton, the scientist who discovered the principles of gravity, also invented the cat flap.

The flat-headed cat is an expert fisher. It has webbed paws to help it swim and well-developed premolars to give it a good grip on slippery prey.

The domestic cat is the only cat species that holds its tail vertically while walking. Wild cats hold their tails horizontally or tucked between their legs.

A cat holding its tail tall

Cats can see brilliantly at dawn and dusk, which are excellent hunting times. They can see well when there is little light because an organ called the "tapetum lucidum" at the back of their eyes reflects light back through the retina. Cats cannot see in complete darkness but they find their way by sound, smell, and the sensitivity of their whiskers.

A cat's ear can turn up to 180 degrees. Each ear has more than 20 muscles that control this movement.

Almost all tortoiseshell cats are female, because the colouring is linked to the female sex gene.

On average, cats spend two-thirds of every day sleeping. So a nine-year-old cat has only been awake for three years of its life.

A cat nap

Cats "meow" often at humans, but hardly ever "meow" at other cats.

The spots on the back of the African cheetah known as the "king cheetah" are so large that they join together to form striking black stripes running down its spine.

A cat cannot see things that are immediately under its nose, because its nose gets in the way.

A person who killed a cat in ancient Egypt could be punished with death.

Relative to its size, the clouded leopard has the biggest canines of all cats. Its sharp, dagger-like teeth can be as long as 4.5 cm (1.8 in).

The average cat-food meal is equivalent to about five mice.

A cat hard at work grooming itself

Cats are extremely clean animals, and spend nearly one-third of their waking hours grooming themselves.

According to Hebrew folklore, God created cats when Noah prayed for help. Noah was afraid that rats would eat all the food he had stored in the ark, so God made the lion sneeze, and out popped a cat.

A cat's colourpoint pattern – where the ears, face, legs, and tail are darker than the main body colour – is affected by temperature. The pattern is caused by a gene that prevents colour in warm parts of the body and allows colour in cooler areas, such as the face, ears and tail. The contrast between the body colour and the point colour is greater in cooler climates because the animal's extremities are cooler.

The clouded leopard

QUESTIONS AND ANSWERS

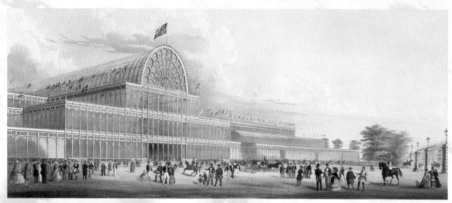

Crystal Palace, London

Q Where was the first formal cat show?

A The first cat show was held at Crystal Palace in London on 13 July 1871.

Q Why does a cat wag its tail?

A A cat will swish its tail when annoyed, will move it more rapidly when very agitated, and will twitch it when excited or curious.

Q How well can a cat smell?

A A cat's sense of smell is so good that it can smell another cat that is 100 m (330 ft) away. Cats smell with their nose, but also use the Jacobson's organ, which is in the roof of a cat's mouth.

Q How many claws does a cat have?

A Most cats have five toes on their front paws and four toes on their back paws. Each toe ends in a sharp claw.

Q What colours are cats' eyes?

A Cats' eyes are often a very striking colour – blue, lavender, yellow, copper, or brilliant orange. Some cats are odd-eyed, with one eye of one colour and one of another. Many pedigree cats are bred to have eyes of a specific colour.

Q How long do cats usually live?

A Healthy cats will normally live for 12 to 15 years, but many live to be 18 or 19 years old.

Cats like rubbing against people

Q Why do cats rub against people's legs?

A When cats rub against people, or against other cats, they are marking them with their scent glands. They often use scent glands that are situated between their eyes and ears, and one near their tail.

Chartreux cats have orange eyes

Q How many teeth do adult cats have?

A Grown cats have a total of 30 teeth, for grasping, cutting, and shredding food. They do not have any teeth for grinding food. Kittens have about 26 temporary teeth, which they lose when they are about six months old.

Q What makes it possible for cats to get through small spaces?

A Cats do not have a true collarbone, so their head is the bulkiest bony structure. Provided they can get their head through first, they can usually manage to squeeze the rest of their body through a very small gap.

Cats can squeeze through small spaces

Record Breakers

● **MOTHER TO THE MOST KITTENS**
A cat called "Dusty" holds the record for producing the largest number of kittens. She had more than 420 kittens in her lifetime, and had her last litter when she was 18 years old.

● **THE WORLD'S BEST "MOUSER"**
"Towser", a tabby working on rodent control in Scotland, caught more mice than any other cat. In her 21 years, she killed an amazing total of 28,899 mice, an average of about four each day.

● **THE LARGEST CAT BREED**
The largest cat breed is the Ragdoll. Male ragdolls weigh between 5.4 and 9 kg (12 to 20 lb), while females weigh between 4.5 and 6.8 kg (10 to 15 lb).

● **THE SMALLEST CAT BREED**
The smallest cat breed is the Singapura. Males weigh about 2.7 kg (6 lb) while females weigh about 1.8 kg (4 lb).

A Singapura kitten

Identifying breeds

THE SELECTIVE BREEDING OF CATS has taken place for more than a century, and during that time the look of the different breeds has changed considerably. Breed standards describe the ideal appearance of a breed, and give guidance on coloration, pattern, and temperament. New breeds result from spontaneous changes, or from the crossing either of two established breeds, or of a domestic cat with a small wild cat.

PEDIGREE OR CROSS-BREED?
A pedigree or pure-bred cat is one whose mother and father belong to the same breed. A non-pedigree, or cross-bred, cat is one whose parents are from different breeds or who are themselves cross-bred.

Mother cat and kittens

HAIR LENGTH

Cats fall into one of three groups, depending on the length of their hair. Long-haired cats have a thick coat that can make them appear twice their actual size. The fur of short-haired cats may be fine or coarse, and the hairs may be straight, crinkled, curly, or wavy. The Sphynx is the only pedigree breed that is "hairless".

The British blue shorthair

The "hairless" Sphynx

The Maine coon, a long-haired cat

COLOURS AND PATTERNS

Over the years, selective breeding has established a variety of different patterns and colours within the recognized breeds.

TABBY COATS are patterned symmetrically with stripes and spots of a dark colour on a lighter background. Tabby colours include blue, brown, cream, red, and silver.

Black

Tortie smoke longhair

SMOKE COATS have a white undercoat covered by guard hairs of a dark colour (usually black, blue, or red).

Silver spotted tabby

SOLID (OR SELF) COATS are of one colour only. The colour may be black, blue (dark grey), brown, cream (tan), lilac (light grey), red (orange), or white.

PARTI-COLOURED COATS have two or more clearly defined colours, such as black and white. Tortoiseshell coats are black, red, and cream, while calico coats are black, white, red, and cream.

Tortie and white

SHADED COATS are similar to smoke coats except that the dark colour occurs only on the tips of the guard hairs.

Red shaded cameo

CAT BREEDS

The Governing Council of the Cat Fancy (GCCF) recognizes the following groups of cat breeds.

PERSIAN LONGHAIRS
With the longest, densest fur of all domestic cats, Persian longhairs need a lot of grooming. They have flat, rounded faces and small ears.

Orange-eyed white Persian longhair.

Cream Turkish van

Cream point British shorthair

BRITISH SHORTHAIRS
Distinguished by the their large, rounded body shape and round faces, there are British shorthairs in a wide range of colours and patterns.

SEMI-LONGHAIRS
Some semi-longhairs, such as the Turkish van, have a thinner undercoat than long-haired cats. Their fur is soft, and silky. Others, such as the Maine coon, have a dense undercoat and a glossy, waterproof top coat.

The strongest point colour is on the tail and the head

FOREIGN CATS
This group includes a range of different cats. The Tiffanie has silky, fine, semi-long hair, and a bushy tail. Asian cats have short, fine, close-lying fur. The ocicat is a relatively new breed that has Siamese and Abyssinian ancestry. The Cornish rex has short, curly hair and a muscular body and legs. The Singapura is a small breed, with a ticked coat.

There are some tabby markings on the face.

BURMESE CATS
Burmese cats have short, glossy fur with a satin feel, muscular bodies, and slender legs. They exist in a range of solid colours, and also tortiseshell.

Red Tiffanie

Cream Burmese

Chocolate point Siamese

ORIENTAL CATS
Oriental shorthairs have short, fine, glossy fur, wedge-shaped faces, and large ears. They have a svelte body, long, slender legs, and a long, tapering tail. The oriental longhair, known as the Angora, has a similar body shape, but long, fine silky fur, with no woolly undercoat.

The ears are big and the nose is long and straight

POINTED COATS
have a solid colour on the main part of the cat's body, and a darker colour on the extremities – the face, ears, legs, feet, and tail.

Lilac oriental shorthair

SIAMESE
Siamese cats also have wedge-shaped faces, long bodies, slender legs, and large, wide ears. All Siamese cats are pointed, having light-coloured bodies with a darker colour on the face, ears, legs, feet, and tail.

TICKED COATS
have bands of colour on each hair, creating a wavy effect.

The back is light blue

Fawn Abyssinian

Blue point Siamese

Find out more

EVEN IF YOU DO NOT HAVE A CAT of your own, there are many ways of finding out more about these attractive, affectionate pets. You could join a cat club and go along to shows. You will meet people who are very knowledgeable about cats, and will find out about the work involved in breeding cats. You could volunteer to help a charity that cares for strays, cats that have been cruelly treated, and cats whose owners can no longer care for them. If big cats are your interest, visit a wildlife park, and see lions, leopards, or tigers in action.

A CAT OF YOUR OWN

If you are considering getting a cat, investigate first the kind of home and care a cat needs. The RSPCA provides information to help you make the decision. The General Council of the Cat Fancy (GCCF) provides details on choosing, feeding, and caring for your kitten. Alternatively, you might decide to rehouse a cat through the RSPCA or another charity.

The judges, dressed in white, examine the cats exhibited at a show

CAT SHOWS

You will learn a lot by going along to a cat show. They take place all year round, usually on Saturdays, and are generally open to the public in the afternoon. Shows vary in size enormously – a small show may have 60 cats competing, while at least 1,500 cats take part in the GCCF Supreme Show, in November each year. A visit to a large show will enable you to find out about many different cat breeds.

Cats belonging to the club may have won many awards

CUTE KITTENS

Breeding pedigree cats is a time-consuming business. The kittens stay with their mother until they are 13 weeks old, and for at least a week after they have completed a vaccination course. This ensures they are fully protected before they go to a new home. Both the kittens and the mother can need a lot of care during this time. At a cat club, you may meet a breeder who is happy for you to visit and learn more about the work involved.

The kitten feels safe near its family

JOIN A CAT CLUB

Find out where your nearest cat club is, and go along. Some clubs are for specific breeds of cat, but many are for all breeds. Clubs organize and take part in shows at which club members can exhibit their cats. There are more than 140 cat clubs in the UK, and the GCCF can provide information and contact details.

Oriental shorthair cats have large ears and a wedge-shaped head

LONG HAIRED SECTION

Places to Visit

THE GOVERNING COUNCIL OF THE CAT FANCY SUPREME CAT SHOW

• Contact the GCCF on www.gccfcats.org.uk to check the location and exact date of this annual November show. Only cats that have won at a GCCF championship show can take part in this Supreme Show, which is for pedigree and non-pedigree cats.

• Cat clubs have information tables and cats on exhibit, so that visitors can learn about the breed of their choice. It can be possible to make arrangements here to visit a breeder in order to choose a kitten.

THE CAT ASSOCIATION OF BRITAIN CAT OF THE YEAR SHOW

• The Cat Association of Britain (CA) is the British member of FIFe , the Fédération Internationale Féline, which spans 37 countries from Russia to Argentina.

• The CA organizes its shows under FIFe rules. The Cat of the Year Show is held in January each year. Check the location and exact date with the CA on www.catassociation.com

• In addition to best cat, kitten and neuter in various categories, there are also awards for best new breed, best household pet, and an award for breeder of the year.

WHIPSNADE WILD ANIMAL PARK, BEDFORDSHIRE, ENGLAND

• Set in 600 acres (240 hectares) of parkland, this is one of Europe's largest conservation parks, with over 2,500 animals. For more information, see www.whipsnade.co.uk/

LONGLEAT SAFARI PARK, WILTSHIRE, ENGLAND

• Opened in 1966, Longleat was the first drive-through safari park outside Africa, situated in the grounds of Longleat House. For further details, go to www.longleat.co.uk/

CATS

One way to find out more about big cats is to go along to wildlife parks, and observe them in action. If you can, talk to one of the keepers. To locate the park that is nearest to you, or to find out which animals are in a certain park, go to the website www.safaripark.co.uk

The animals are used to visitors in their cars.

STRAY CATS

Sadly, some people get a cat without really considering whether they can care for it. Others are cruel to their cats. Charities that take care of injured and stray cats welcome volunteers, to help care for the cats and find suitable new homes for them. Cats Protection has a total of 9,000 volunteers, who help to rehouse about 60,000 cats each year. The RSPCA also rescues and rehouses large numbers of cats and kittens.

USEFUL WEBSITES

• For information on the Governing Council of the Cat Fancy, see www.gccfcats.org.uk

• To find details of the Cat Association of Britain, go to www.catassociation.com

• For a wealth of information on pedigree cats in the UK, with sections on breeds, breeders, cat clubs, and cat shows, go to www.palantir.co.uk/gccf.html

• To find out about the PDSA, a charity that provides a free veterinary service for the sick and injured pets of needy people, see www.pdsa.org.uk/pages/index

• For information on Cats Protection, go to www.cats.org.uk/

• Find out about the work of the Royal Society for the Protection of Animals at www.rspca.org.uk

• For information on responsible pet ownership, go to www.bbc.co.uk/nature/animals/pets/responsible.shtml

• For a wealth of information about big cats, see www.bornfree.org.uk/

• Find a fact file on each of the big cats on www.bbc.co.uk/nature/reallywild/wildfacts/

Glossary

AWN HAIRS Bristly hairs with thickened tips. Awn hairs are longer than down hairs, but not as long as guard hairs.

BREED A group of cats with particular characteristics. Humans control breeding to achieve specific features, such as coat type or head shape. If the breeding is not strictly supervised, characteristics can very quickly be lost.

BREED STANDARD The official description of a breed, setting out size, weight, colour, etc.

BRINDLE A mix of tan and black hair.

CAMOUFLAGE The coloration of an animal that either blends in with the colour of the surroundings or breaks up the animal's outline with stripes or spots, making it harder to see. Camouflage can be important both for animals that hunt and those that are hunted.

The four large canine teeth

CANINE TEETH Four large, pointed teeth, two in the upper and two in the lower jaw. Some cats kill their prey by stabbing them with their canine teeth.

CARNASSIAL TEETH The teeth at the side of the cat's jaw that are used for cutting off meat.

CARNIVORE A member of the order Carnivora, which contains animals that have teeth specialized for biting and shearing flesh. Most carnivores live primarily on meat.

CATERWAUL A howling, wailing cry made by a female cat when it is on heat.

CLASS Any of the taxonomic groups into which a phylum is divided. A class contains one or more orders. Cats are part of the class Mammalia.

CLAW A curved, sharp, pointed attachment to the toe. Cats draw in, or retract, their claws when they are relaxed, but can extend them quickly when necessary. The cheetah is the only cat that cannot retract its claws.

COBBY Having a short, compact body shape.

CROSS-BREEDING The mating of two different breeds.

DOUBLE COAT A coat made up of a long top-coat over a short undercoat.

DOWN HAIR The soft, fine hair that makes up a short undercoat and provides body insulation.

FAMILY Any of the taxonomic groups into which an order is divided. A family contains one or more genera. Felidae is the name of the cat family.

FELINE Cat or catlike.

FERAL CATS Domestic cats that have returned to living in the wild and live totally outside human control.

FOLD A cat with ears that fold and turn down.

FORELEGS The front legs of a four-legged animal.

GENUS (plural **GENERA**) Any of the taxonomic groups into which a family is divided. A genus contains one or more species.

GROOM To keep clean and tidy. People groom cats, but cats also spend considerable time grooming themselves with their tongues and paws.

A feral cat

Grooming a cat at a show

GUARD HAIRS Long hairs that form part of the top-coat.

HABITAT The natural home of an animal or plant.

HIND LEGS The back legs of a four-legged animal.

INBREEDING Repeated breeding within a group of animals that are closely related to each other. Inbreeding can cause mutations.

JACOBSON'S ORGAN A taste-smell organ in the roof of a cat's mouth.

KITTEN A young cat. The young of some large cats are known as cubs.

LIGAMENT The tough tissue that connects bones and cartilage, and that supports muscle.

LITTER A group of young born at one time to one female cat.

LONGHAIR A cat with a thick, long, double coat.

MANE Long hair growing on or around the neck.

MOULT To lose hair so that new growth can take place. Cats moult especially in the spring when they lose the thick coat they had for the winter.

MUTATION A change in the genetic make-up resulting in an alteration in the appearance of an animal.

NEUTER A cat that has been either castrated (if a male) or spayed (if a female). Neutered cats often form a separate category in cat shows.

NOSE LEATHER The area of coloured skin, not covered by fur, on a cat's nose.

ORDER Any of the taxonomic groups into which a class is divided. An order contains one or more families. Cats belong to the order Carnivora.

PADS The leathery areas with no hair on the feet.

PAPILLAE The hard, shiny points on a cat's tongue, used to lap up water, and for grooming.

PARTI-COLOURED A cat with a coat of two or more clearly defined colours.

PAW A cat's foot, with its leathery pads and sharp claws.

PEDIGREE The record of a pure-breed's ancestors.

PHYLUM A major taxonomic division of living organisms. A phylum contains one or more classes. Cats belong to the phylum Chordata, which includes animals that have backbones (known as the vertebrates).

POINTS Darker coloured areas at the body's extremities – on the legs, paws, tail, head, and ears.

PURE-BREED A cat with parents belonging to the same breed. A pure-breed is also known as a pedigree cat.

PURR To make a low, vibrant sound, usually expressing pleasure. The sound is made when the bones at the base of the tongue vibrate. Domestic cats and other small cats purr, whereas most large cats can only roar.

SELF (or **SOLID**) A cat with a coat of one colour only.

SEMI-LONGHAIR A cat with a relatively long top-coat, but a fairly thin undercoat.

A cat's tongue is covered in papillae

SHORTHAIR A cat with a short coat.

SKELETON The framework of bones that gives shape to an animal, provides anchorage for muscles, protects vital organs, is a source of blood cells, and provides a mineral store.

SMOKE A cat with a white undercoat and a darker top-coat.

SPECIES Any of the taxonomic groups into which a genus is divided. Members of the same species are able to breed with each other.

SPHYNX A breed of cat that is hairless apart from a little short, downy fur, mainly on its extremities.

SPRAYING Using urine to mark a territory. Tom cats that have not been castrated do this particularly.

STALKING To approach prey stealthily and quietly.

TAPETUM LUCIDUM The cells at the back of a cat's eye that reflect light. The tapetum lucidum makes it possible for a cat to see well when there is not a lot of light.

TAXONOMY Relating to the classification of organisms into groups, based on their similarities or origin.

TENDON A band of tough tissue that attaches a muscle to a bone.

TICKED A coat in which there are bands of different colour on each hair.

TOM A male cat.

A Turkish van pedigree cat

TOP-COAT The outer coat of a cat, made up of the guard hairs and awn hairs.

TORTOISESHELL A cat with black, and light and dark red markings. Tortoiseshell cats are usually female.

UNDERCOAT (or **UNDERFUR**) The dense, soft fur beneath the outer, coarser fur in some mammals.

VAN A coat with a white body but a coloured head and tail.

WEAN When a kitten changes from a milk diet to a meat diet.

WHISKERS The stiff hairs known as tactile hairs that grow on a cat's face. Whiskers are attached to nerves that send messages to the brain when the whiskers touch things.

A mother cat suckles her kittens

SHEATHE To allow a claw to move back inside the bony, protective structure known as a sheath.

SUCKLE To suck milk from the mother. The term also means to give milk to a young animal.

TABBY A coat with striped, blotched, spotted, or ticked markings.

Index

Acknowledgements

Dorling Kindersley would like to thank:
Trevor Smith and all the staff at Trevor Smith's Animal World; Jim Clubb of Clubb-Chipperfield; Nicki Barrass of A1 Animals; Terry Moore of the Cat Survival Trust; the staff of the British Museum and the Natural History Museum for their assistance; Jacquie Gulliver and Lynne Williams for their work on the initial stages of the book; Christian Sévigny and Liz Sephton for design assistance; Claire Gillard and Céline Carez for editorial assistance.

Picture credits
The publisher would like to thank the following for their kind permission to reproduce their photographs:
a=above t=top b=bottom l=left r=right c=centre
Animals Unlimited: 53b; Ardea: R.Beames 40c; K. Fink 40tr; Bridgeman Art Library: back jacket bl above, 28tc, 62tl; Bibliothèque Nationale, Paris 28tb; Chadwick Gallery, Warwicks 52c; National Gallery, London 30tl detail; National Gallery of Scotland 54bl; Victoria & Albert Museum, London 20tl; Courtesy of the Trustees of the British Museum: 6tr, 22bl, 31tr; In the Collection of the Duke of Buccleuch & Queensberry KT: 16cr detail; Jean Loup Charmet: 7tr; Bruce Coleman Ltd: 57tr; Jen & Des Bartlett 13c, 23bl, 25c, 28c; Jane Burton 16cb; Jane Burton & Kim Taylor 16cl; Eric Creighton 26cl; Gerald Cubitt 39br, 43b; G. D. Plage 24cl; Hans Reinhard 12c, 16tl, 24bl, 37tc, 42-43; Norman Tomalin 45bl; Konrad Wothe 22br; Rod Williams 11c, 33cb; Gunter Ziesler 42c, 43tl; E.T. Archive: 24tr, 62br, © Sheila Roberts 1971, 63tc; Mary Evans Picture Library: 10cl, 19t, 27cr, 49tl, tr, 58br; Werner Forman Archive: 33b, 35tr;

Freer Gallery of Art, Washington: 21tl detail, Acc. No. 04.357; Robert Harding Picture Library: 49bl; Marc Henrie: 50cl; "Mr & Mrs Clark & Percy" 1970-1, © David Hockney/photo Tate Gallery: 54tl; Michael Holford: front jacket tr & tl below, 31tl, c, 35b, 37c, 47tr, 47br, 48cl; Hulton-Deutsch Collection: 30b; Hutchison Library: 34c; Image Bank: 54cl; Images Colour Library: 47bl, 48tl, 58tl; Kobal Collection: 11cl, 22t, 49cr; M.R. Long: 9c; LYNX: 36tr; Mansell Collection: 13bl; Metropolitan Museum of Art: 57b; Museum of American Folk Art: 52t; National Gallery of Art, Washington: 55tr (gift of Edgar William & Bernice Chrysler Garbisch); Natural History Museum: 8tl, bl, 12bl, 13tl, br, 33c, 35c, 36cr, 37c, 38c; Natural History Photographic Agency: Agence Nature 18bl; Anthony Bannister 42b; Nigel Dennis 45tl; Patrick Fagot 19c; Peter Johnson 14cl, 45cl; Stephen Krasman 16tr; Gérard Lacz 12tl, 58tr, 59bl; Northampton Historical Society, Mass.: 15tc; Oxford Scientific Films: 37tl, 39tl; Roy Coombes 27c; Sean Morris 41b; Richard Packwood 12cb; Kjell Sandved 59br; Bernard

Schellhammer 53cr; Quadrant Picture Library: 42cb; Courtesy of The Savoy: 51cr; Scala: Palazzo Medici Riccardi, Florence 32bl detail; Museo Nationale, Napoli 46tl; National Museum, Athens 47tl; Spectrum Colour Library: 8br; Frank Spooner Pictures: 61br; Survival Anglia; Dieter & Mary Plage 32tl; Alan Root 27tr; Maurice Tibbles 14tr; Amoret Tanner: 28tc; Victoria & Albert Museum Picture Library: 43tr detail; Zefa: 16ct; E. & P. Bauer 23bl, 38bl; M. N. Boulton 11bl; Bramaz 63br; G. Dimijian 21cr; D. Kessel 35tl; Lummerc 20br; Orion 19cb Ardea London Ltd: John Daniels 64tl, 68crb; Masahiro Iijima 64br; Corbis: Tom Brakefield 66–67; Roy Morsch 68–69; John Periam /Cordaiy Photo Library Ltd 69bc; DK Images: Gables 70–71; Jerry Young 70bc; Longleat Safari Park, Wiltshire: 69clb; Oxford Scientific Films: Richard Packwood 71tc; Rex Features: John Gooch 68–69tc.
Philip Berry;Frank lane picture agency 65-65
All other images © Dorling Kindersley
Illustrations by: Dan Wright